Bright Ideas

For Australian Cake Decorating

By Gail Dorter

Photography by
Stephanie Barnes

Bright Ideas

For Australian Cake Decorating

Design & Co-Ordination:
Artworks & Publishing
PO Box 328, Leederville, Western Australia, 6907

Typesetting, Colour Separations, Pre-Press:
Typestyle Pty. Ltd.
9 Robertson Street, East Perth, Western Australia, 6004

Plates & Printing:
Lamb Print Pty. Ltd.
9 Robertson Street, East Perth, Western Australia, 6004

Photography:
Stephanie Barnes

Author/Publisher:
Gail Dorter
PO Box 79, Hillarys, Western Australia, 6923

Copyright ©:
Gail Dorter: 1994

National Library of Australia
ISBN 0 646 20363 0.

It is necessary in a book of this type to name all the flowers described
within. Many are indeed life-like, while some bear only a passing
resemblance to their namesakes. I hope "Mother Nature" will forgive me.
All the Cakes, Flowers & Ornamental Pieces described and/or pictured
in this book are the sole work of the Author, Gail Dorter.

Contents

Cover Story I created this medium oval cake for a small
wedding celebration, but with minor additions and alterations,
have used the same design for other occasions. By adding a third
candle (for the Holy Trinity) and replacing the rings with a
name, it was perfect for an adult baptism. To make it suit a ruby
wedding celebration, I simply replaced the bible with another
Rose, and piped an appropriate message in the centre. The spray
consists of full red Roses and buds, purple Mock Agapanthus
(the perfect colour to avoid the "Christmas Cake" look), and a
few white small flowers, plus red edged leaves and plenty of
satin ribbon loops. The whole arrangement – including the
candles – was made on an edible disc. To create a contrast
between the bible and the cake, I brushed the bible fairly heavily
with mother of pearl hi-liter, so that it had a slightly luminous
glow. The side decoration consists of six piped and flooded
sprays of open roses, plus flooded lace above a 1cm wide satin
ribbon at the base. A white satin ribbon circles the flooded board.

About the Author

It is seven years since the publication of Gail's first book "CUTTER CLASS Flowers for Australian Cake Decorating", and apart from making many new friends, she says not much has changed in that time. Life still consists of designing and making cakes, floristry, home duties, and fishing if time and weather permit. Since publishing her second book "A TOUCH OF CLASS for Australian Cake Decorating", Gail has visited and demonstrated in Japan and the UK. While in England she was honoured with an invitation to demonstrate at the prestigious "Sugarcraft 93" in Telford. Of her Japanese trip she says "Although I speak no Japanese and many of the students had no knowledge of English, once the demonstrations started it was obvious that the love of sugarcraft was all we needed to be able to communicate with each other".

With the publication of BRIGHT IDEAS behind her, Gail hopes to find more time to spend in the garden, writing to the friends she has made overseas, and maybe even catch a really big fish. As she puts it "Time to smell the roses, not just make them!".

Introduction

I am essentially a cake decorator, so when making flowers, leaves or nuts, I concern myself more with their artistic merits, rather than a precise number of petals or stamens. Producing botanically correct blooms is the realm of the horticulturist and mother nature.

My interest lies in creating the representation of a flower, so that it is not only recognisable to my clients, but which is easily made and arranged, as well as looking attractive and appropriate on a cake.

To the same end, I don't always arrange leaves and flowers in the same configuration you would find in nature, but rather in a way that pleases the eye, and will compliment the style or shape of the cake in question.

This also applies to colour and size. There is simply no point in making a flower perfect in size and colour, if it then overwhelms the cake, or clashes with the bridesmaids dresses. I believe this attitude is called "artistic licence", and you will see that I have taken great advantage of it in this book.

Terms used to describe techniques used

FLUTE Rest the petal(s) on your index finger. Hold the fluting tool between the thumb and first three fingers of the other hand, and with a "roll and press" action, work backwards and forwards around the petal. If you are used to fluting with the petals resting on a board, you will find that by resting them on your fingers you will have more control, and they will finish by curling ever so slightly back. Practice makes perfect!

MOVEMENT To lift and slightly twist petal (*as opposed to frilling them*). Rest the petal on your index finger. Hold the fluting tool between the thumb and first three fingers of the other hand, and roll it very firmly forwards only, around the petal.

FINGER EDGES Use your thumb and fingers to gently smooth and flatten out rough edges, and where required, to rub chalk colouring into petals. If you are planning to dip-colour flowers, then smooth edges are essential, as the colour will accentuate the slightest roughness.

PAINT CALYX Thin some royal icing with water, or melted moulding paste (*see page 10*), and colour it. Use a brush, suitably sized for the flower under construction, to paint a calyx on to the back of the flower. This not only holds the flower firmly on its stem, but when fixed into sprays, that little extra bit of green adds a natural look to arrangements. Because the flowers are neatly and realistically finished, it is not necessary to hide the backs of them, so quite often, fewer flowers are needed.

CURL THE EDGES Place the flower on thick (*my foam is 2 inches thick*), soft foam, and using a ball tool, gently press and pull towards the centre of the flower. Curl each petal separately, and always start at the very edge, and stop before reaching the centre of the flower.

POLLEN Pollen adds a softening look to icing flowers, and is easily made. Simply put fresh desiccated coconut through a blender, then sift out and keep the finest particles. One teaspoon of this is sufficient for dozens of small blossoms. It can be tinted to any colour using scraped chalks, Petal Dust,

or liquid colours. *One note of warning though* – if you put the coconut through the blender too long, it will be reduced to an oily consistency – totally unsuitable. There are many other foodstuffs that can be used as pollen, but coconut is the only one that is white, and therefore can be tinted to any colour. There are now also commercially made "Pollens" available.

STAMENS There are literally dozens of different sizes, styles and colours of stamens now available for cake decorators. I use basically three different sizes, and usually buy white, which can be dipped in alcohol mix to achieve any colour I want. If you are just beginning on cutter flowers, and are using stamens as the stems, use the large stamens until you become adept at pulling them through without the flower sliding back down the stem. You will notice when looking through this book that I also use a lot of the superfine Japanese stamens. While they are more expensive, and fiddly to handle, they are worth the extra bother and expense, as flowers using them always look more delicate and natural *(especially small blooms)*.

WIRE I use very thin non rusting florists' wire, and in most cases cover it with white or green florists' tape before inserting it in the flowers. Where there is a chance that the tape on a wire may show in the centre of a flower, then I tape initially in white, and overtape with green *(if required)* when the flower is finished.

TAPING WIRE The beauty of taping your own wire is that you can have exactly the grade of wire you require in exactly the shade or colour your want. If done properly, it doesn't peel back off the wire the way the cotton and paper covered wires do, and adds very little extra bulk to the wires. As well, when you tape your flowers into a spray, everything matches. There are two different types of tape - PARAFILM, which is smooth, and should be stretched over the wire, and STEMTEX, which is rather like sticky crepe paper. I prefer the PARAFILM, which among other benefits, will enable you to pull the stem easily out of a finished flower, so that you can glue it directly on to a cake. It comes in green, white, and brown, and using it can be mastered with only a little practice. For the thin wires that we usually use, it it best to split the tape into two, or even three for very fine wire *(28g and 30g)*. Always start with a pulled end of tape. Hold the wire in your left hand, the tape in your right.

Lay the wire over the end of the tape, and spin the wire between your fingers to wrap the tape around. Once the first bit is caught, pull the tape at a fortyfive degree angle away from the wire with your right hand, stretching it to about double its length, then twist the wire down the tape. Continue stretching the tape, then twisting the wire down it, to the end, then break off the tape. STEMTEX is used in virtually the same way, except that it doesn't have the same stretch, and therefore tends to add extra thickness to the wire. While it comes in different shades of green that can be very useful, its stickiness can cause it to pick up any stray chalk or petal dust, and the white can look quite grubby by the time you have wired a spray together. Pulling the stems out of completed flowers is not quite so easy if you have used STEMTEX, but it is not impossible either.

EDIBLE DISCS These are green, slightly transparent, edible discs on which sprays can be mounted before placing them on a cake. They have two "lugs" on the underside, which enables you to remove a spray from a cake, then replace it in exactly the same position. The lugs also stop the disc from turning or moving on the cake as you arrange your flowers. They come in various sizes, and one or more can be joined together, by firstly cutting off the raised lip that surrounds them, moistening the parts that are to overlap, then twisting the two pieces while simultaneously pressing them together. Discs can also be bent to go round the sides or top edges of cakes, but again the raised lip should be cut off with scissors first. To use a disc, firstly decide where on the cake it is to go, and press it, lugs down, into the icing. Next, moisten the top of the disc slightly, and form a wad of icing on top of it, bringing it smoothly to the edges. Now it is just a matter of inserting the flowers and ribbons, safe in the knowledge that the wires are not actually penetrating the cake, and the entire spray can easily be lifted off for safekeeping. By wiring a trailer separately, then adding it into the the arrangement, you will have what looks just like a wired bouquet, without the need to take floristry lessons. Left-over flowers can also be utilised by arranging them on a disc *(lugs upwards, and remove the lip)*. When you are asked to perform your next miracle and produce a cake overnight, simply take the disc with the pre-arranged spray on it, fill the lug holes with royal icing, place it on the cake, and presto – instant decoration. You will need to slide a knife under the disc to remove it if you use it in this fashion, but they come away fairly easily. If you require a cascade effect in the floral arrangement, use the disc for arranging the central flowers, then remove the wires from those remaining, and glue them directly on to the cake.

REMOVING WIRES FROM FINISHED FLOWERS
To remove the wires from finished flowers, hold them firmly by the calyx, and with your free hand, grip the wire firmly, *(you may need to use pliers)*, give it a slight twist, and apply steady pressure – don't yank at it. If you have used Parafilm for your taping, then the wire will come away fairly easily. If you have used a hooked or bent over wire in the construction of the flower, then you will not be able to remove it, so plan ahead when first designing the cake.

The Autumn tones on this cream, two tier hexagonal cake, were inspired by the burnt orange colour of the bridesmaids' dresses. The bride requested Open Roses in champagne, but also wanted orange to be a feature. Rather than have small spots of deep colour dotted through the sprays, I chose to make the leaves in Autumn tones (I started with pale green leaves, brushed deep orange on the tips and side edges, then brushed a darker green down the centre before steaming). Crowea with deep orange tips (I used fine blank stamens and tipped them myself) were a subtle re-inforcement of colour. The addition of plenty of long ribbon loops in cream helped to soften the arrangements, as well as creating a change of texture. A simple border of dropped loops, plus two rings, and flooded boards with cream satin ribbon trim complete the picture. The cakes were 10" and 6", and the twist acrylic pillars 3" tall.

Tools

Holed Board

To successfully create flowers from cutters you will need a few basic tools.

A piece of SOFT FOAM, which should be of fine consistency, kept free of little grains of icing, and most importantly, at least TWO INCHES thick. BALL TOOLS of various sizes. I use such items as dressmakers pin heads, curler pins, swizzle sticks, and a melon baller – as well as commercially made ball tools.

You will also need a FLUTING TOOL, such as a short length of knitting needle, the end of a paint brush, or a curler pin for small flowers. Again, there are commercialy produced tools available. A length of plastic piping makes an excellent ROLLING PIN, but if you can afford it, there are excellent non-stick ones in the shops. Something flat and smooth to roll the paste out on is a must. I have an acrylic board which was purchased as a "scrap" from a plastics retailer. Vinyl place mats are also excellent, especially if you have metal cutters that tend not to cut properly – the vinyl has some give, so the cutters generally work better. Once again though, if you are prepared to pay a little extra there are excellent non-stick boards available. A good pair of long TWEEZERS are a must for inserting stamens, lifting flowers, and arranging them in sprays.

It is necessary to rest the flowers in or on something until they are dry. Small flowers with stamens as stems can be pushed into florists foam (OASIS). For larger flowers, you can utilise egg cartons, or cardboard fruit trays. Better still, try making a HOLED BOARD.

Holed boards (*flower stands*) are essential for cutter flowers, and handy for pulled ones. They allow flowers to dry while holding their shape, and are invaluable if you are transporting them any distance. They are neither difficult nor expensive to make.

Many materials can be used. As long as it is approximately 5 or 6 millimetres (*1/4inch*) thick, and able to be drilled, it is suitable.

Cut the board to the size you feel you need, mark where the holes are be be, and with a 6.35mm (*1/4inch*) bit, drill the initial holes. Use a counter sinking tool to round them out, and if necessary, sandpaper any rough spots. Add legs, and it is ready for use.

If you are not able or prepared to make your own boards, then there are excellent commercially made ones now available. They come with different sized holes, and even with folding legs for easy storage.

HOLED BOARD

Moulds

Stamens on stems

Many flowers need to be made in a mould to help establish their shape. It is possible to buy some commercially made forms, but it is easy and inexpensive to make your own.

Firstly, transfer the pattern from below on to a piece of stiff cardboard, or soft plastic, such as the lid of an icecream or margarine container. Cut them out.

Prepare some leftover moulding paste, or childrens putty (*purchased from a toy store*), by pressing it into a small container, or simply make it into a block.

Gently form a hole in the centre, then use the pattern piece as a guide for the correct shape, turning it so the hole is even. The finished mould should correspond with the pattern. Round off the edges, and set aside to dry thoroughly. If you wish to preserve your mould it can be painted or sealed.

Use a ball tool to form the initial hole for Azalia or Godetia moulds, and an icing tube (*nozzle*) for the lilly mould. If you wish to make bigger flowers, it is a simple matter to build larger moulds.

As well as these moulds, holed boards or flower stands can be used to form many flowers in, along with very small funnels. I also find the Wilton Lily Nails very useful for cupped or bell shaped flowers. If you use double thickness alfoil when making cups in the Lily Nails they are very strong, and can be used any number of times.

All flowers are easier to arrange if they are on a stem, so incorporating the centre of the flower with a stem makes sense.

Cut the stamens to the required length, and hold them in your right hand, with the stamens side by side, and the cut ends level. Rest a piece of florists tape across your left index finger, and lay the stamens over the tape, about 0.5cm (1/4") from the end. Use your left thumb to fold the end of the tape over the stamens, then roll them up tightly. Once secure, insert a length of wire next to the stamens and continue taping down the length of the wire. Don't simply "bandage" the wire. The correct way is to twist the wire with your left hand, while gently stretching the tape with your right hand, and pulling it away from the wire at a 45 degree angle. You may find it easier if you cut the tape to half its width. It is also wise to use white tape for this, as it will not show through as a dark spot in the centre of the flower, and if you require a green stem, then you can always over-tape with green after the flower is finished. If you are making flowers that require very fine tips, and therefore plan to use blank stamens, cut the tips off after you have taped them to the wire – they are easier to hold and work with if the tips are intact. Very thin royal icing makes excellent tips, but for extremely small flowers just a little dab of straight colour on very fine stamens will create an extremely delicate look.

Karume Azalia

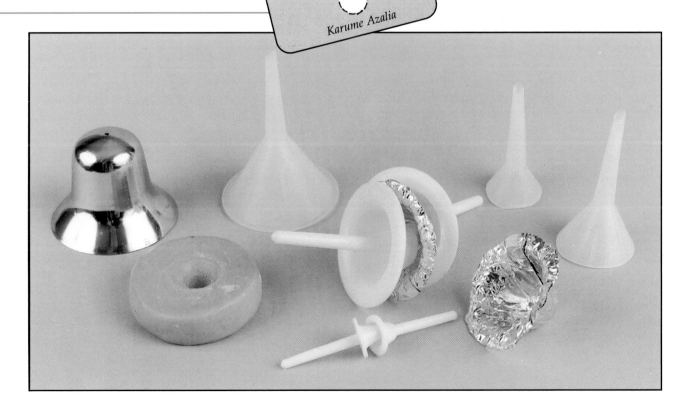

Melted Moulding Paste

The idea of melting moulding paste came to me some years ago, when on the eve of a prestigious show I broke a petal off a vital flower in an arrangement. It had to be fixed quickly, and preferably invisibly. I knew it would be difficult matching the colour of the flower in royal icing, so decided to melt some left-over moulding paste. It worked beautifully, but it was so fiddly trying to melt a tiny bit of paste in a double boiler that the idea was shelved. However, since I have discovered the magic of microwaves, I have realised what a great idea it was.

The method is simple. Put a small amount of paste into a tiny container (*I use a plastic pill dispenser kept from a hospital stay*), add several drops of water, and zap for a few seconds. You need to watch and catch it before it boils, or you will have toffee. It must be stirred well, and then used fairly quickly before it sets. Sitting the container in hot water will help, and it can also be put back in the microwave once more, but again, don't let it boil.

If by this time you are feeling deprived because you don't have a microwave oven, then read on, as there is a simple way of melting paste without one. Simply fill a small jar (*I use a Vegemite jar*) with boiling water. Find another small container that will sit in the mouth of the first jar and touch the water. Place your paste and a few drops of water into the top container and cover it with a lid for a minute or so, after which time, all it will need is a little stirring before use.

As I stated previously, it is ideal for repair work, as it dries quickly and blends in perfectly. It is useful on flowers that are to be dipped, because not only is it less affected by the moisture than royal icing is, but being of the same medium as the basic flower, it accepts the colour to the same density.

Remember that melted moulding paste is stronger than royal icing, so keep it in mind for all the fiddly little things you do, such as joining up models (*baby bassinets, wheelbarrows, churches etc*). A great hint I was given at a recent seminar is to tie a small piece of paste and a drop or two of water into the corner of a plastic bag before melting it. Roll the bag

Melted Moulding Paste
Continued

between your fingers to mix the water and paste well, then cut a tiny hole in the corner of the bag, and pipe the paste along the join lines of whatever you are building. If you then use a damp brush to smooth over any bulges of paste, once dried, you will have a near invisible join. Melted paste is also ideal if you are trying to attach anything to the side of a cake.

One more tip which you may find useful if you are using powder colours to tint some paste. Melt a small amount of your paste, *(minus the water)*, then add the powder, and stir well. The heat from the paste will burst the little colour buds, and you will have maximum colouration, which means no horrible spotting or streaking. Keep stirring the paste as it cools, then work it into your moulding paste a little at a time, till you have the depth of colour you require. You may have to let the finished paste rest a few minutes before you use it, but it is still far quicker than the conventional method.

Tylose Glue

1/4 teaspoon Tylose powder sprinkled on 50 mls water

I have mentioned "glue" in quite a number of places in this book, and like most people I have my preference for the type of glue I use. Until recently I stuck to plain egg white, but for a number of reasons, now use the tylose glue. It is made by dropping a small amount of Tylopure powder *(tylose)* into water, and allowing it to soak. There is no real recipe as such, because it depends just how thick you want it. I regularly add a little extra water if I am doing a job that requires a thin glue, but quite happily add a pinch more powder if I need a really thick glue - such as when painting tips on stamens. If you keep your glue fairly thick, then it doesn't actually wet the icing you paint it on, and flowers dry that much quicker, and hold their shape better. It also has the advantage of not going "off" quite as readily as egg white.

Tylose powder can be used rather than for glue. Mixed into Petinice or Regalice at the rate of approximately 1 tsp to 250 grams, and worked in well, it makes Garrett frills and continuous lace borders much easier to handle. This same mix also makes an excellent medium for plaques. By making it just a little stronger it is ideal for wheelbarrows and such. When it comes to forming arrangements on edible discs, I work about 1/4 tsp of Tylose into a desertspoon of fondant, and then use the Tylose glue to stick it to the disc. This mix will set very quickly, so your flowers readily sit where you place them, and the whole spray will be very stable.

The roses and purple Mock Agapanthus in this arrangement were dipped, while the leaves were made a medium green, then chalked with darker green and the edges touched up with deep bergundy, before being steamed.

Colouring with Chalks or Petal Dust

Colouring and highlighting icing flowers with chalks or petal dust is easy and effective, particularly if the chalking is later "set" by steaming or dipping. Regardless of whether you use scraped chalks or petal dust, you will find you get better results if you mix a little potato flour with your colour. By mixing various amounts of it with your colour medium you will find that streaking is eliminated, and it is easier to achieve gradual shading. Even the pearly hi-liters are easier to use creatively with a little potato flour mixed into them.

On large flowers, chalking is done first, before any shaping and while the icing is soft. Dust on the powdered chalk with a soft brush, blow or brush off any excess, then blend it into the icing with your thumb. It is essential to do this first if petals are to overlap. Flowers done this way can be highlighted with extra colour once dried.

For dry flowers use a soft, flat brush, dip it in the chalk, and drag the flat side of the brush across the edge of the petals, Some of the chalk will flick off onto the petals, but you will find the colour is concentrated on the edge, and fades in towards the centre. Shake off any excess. If you want intense colour on just the very edge, hold the flower upside down so the chalk can't fall back on the petals. You can add a deep red edge to rose leaves with this method. Small flowers on stems can be simply dipped into a container of colour, and any excess powder blown off.

It is not necessary to buy dozens of different chalks or dusts, as they are easily mixed and blended. With just a few basic colours you can create almost any hue. If you are stuck for a particular shade, then try dipping white chalk in liquid colour. Once it has dried it can be used in the normal way. To turn bright pink into a soft dusky colour, add a scrape of green. To take the harsh tone off yellow, add a little pink. A lot of colours can be deepened with a tiny bit of black. If you have difficulty matching up a fabric colour, try separating a few threads. Quite often the material will be made of two or three different coloured threads woven together, and you can use them as a guide to mixing a matching chalk.

Just remember to always add potato flour, and only a little colour at a time when mixing new shades.

For a perfect finish to chalked flowers, "set" the colours by steaming or dipping them.

The original concept for this cake for Sarah was to have the baby under the proverbial cabbage leaf, but as cabbage leaves are ugly and cumbersome, I used artistic licence and changed it to a somewhat glamourised spinach leaf. A mould was used for the baby's face, the rest was made freehand. Once dry, a little of the same paste was melted and thinned, then painted over all the joins for a smoother more natural finish. A pink hair bow and dummy were also added (a blue bib and dummy would be appropriate for a boy). The roses in the spray were tinted to match the baby's skin colour. The Daisies were dipped mauve, with a yellow pollen centre added last. The tiny white Eriostemon also have pollen centres. Thinned pink royal icing was used to flood the extension base, with matching pink lace as the finishing touch.

Colouring by Dipping

Colouring icing flowers by the dipping method is not only easy, but leaves the finished flowers with a natural, slightly translucent look. It is perfect for deep colours, where often by the time you have achieved the colour you want in your paste the texture has so changed that it is almost impossible to work with. Leftover flowers can be over-dipped to a deeper shade, or even a completely different colour. By making all your flowers in white, then dipping them, you will avoid having lots of little bits of coloured paste that eventually dry up and are wasted.

The technique of dipping works around the principle that alcohol dries very quickly, and so, if the alcohol is coloured, anything dipped in it will dry very quickly, leaving behind an even coat of colour.

Obviously, the higher the alcoholic content of the dip, the quicker the flower will dry, and the better

the result will be. Pure alcohol is perfect, but unfortunately, not always available. Here in Western Australia it is possible to buy natural cooking concentrate Vodka, which has an 80% alcohol volume, but if you are unable to purchase a similar product, then check on some of the clear liqueurs available at your local liquor outlet. Polish Spirits is an excellent substitute, *(though more expensive)*, and has the advantage of being drinkable should you fancy a tipple *(unlike the concentrate)*.

The actual technique is simple - hold the flower by the stem, dip it in the prepared solution, then spin the flower to flick off the excess liquid, leaving nice even coloration. If you follow a few basic rules, you can colour flowers beautifully, and easily.

Firstly, for really good results, you need to add some copha *(solidified oil)* to your paste. *(Some recipes include copha, in which case it is not necessary to add any*

Colouring by Dipping

extra). Simply take a small amount of copha, and work it well into the paste before beginning your flowers.

Obviously you need something to hold on to, so a decent stem is a must.

Even though the alcohol solution dries very quickly, it still wets the flowers, so they must be thoroughly dry, and all petals must be securely attached before you begin. To this end, it is best to use thinned melted moulding paste where you would normally use royal icing, as it is less affected by moisture. Royal icing also absorbs the colour at a different rate to moulding paste, and you can find that flowers will have darker patches where the royal icing is.

Have your mix in containers wide enough, and deep enough to accommodate the flowers you are dipping. Dip them in long enough to wet them, but not soak them till they start to sag.

Have a large empty container handy and twirl the flowers within it, unless of course you wish to redecorate your walls and furniture, not to mention yourself. A piece of foam in the bottom is advisable, as sooner or later you will drop a flower, and it may survive a soft landing.

If you want a white centre, or perhaps to keep the original colour on a central stamen *(as in violets),* then paint the parts you don't wish coloured with melted copha before dipping.

If you want a rich deep colour, such as red or bergundy, then add powder, rather than liquid colour to the alcohol.

Remember when mixing colours that they will tend to dry a little darker than they appear when wet. Save any broken or unsuitable flowers for testing colours on, and let one dry first, before going ahead and perhaps being sorry later.

Have a container of clear alcohol handy, as if you realise that a colour is really wrong, you can remove much of it by quickly swishing the flower in clear alcohol. It will need to dry before you can re-dip it to the corrected colour.

If you want a highlight effect, such as a darker centre or tips, then you can chalk it on first, or paint it with a deeper alcohol mix before dipping.

Flowers that have pollen in them should be dipped before finishing off. Also remember that if you use coloured stamens they will be even darker once dipped, and may alter the overall colour of the finished flower.

If you are colouring really big flowers, then they can be quickly and liberally washed with solution using your biggest brush, then twirled as usual.

As the alcohol can be expensive, only mix small amounts at a time, and use containers with good seals for storage, to minimise evaporation.

Be very careful steaming dipped flowers. As the colour is only a thin coating over the icing, it can very easily finish with a mottled look if you are heavy handed with steaming. Dipped flowers, with the translucent look that it creates, are rarely improved by steaming anyway.

So, if you haven't already tried it, buy yourself some alcohol, and start experimenting with all those old flowers you have made and never used.

Steaming

In order to give finished flowers and leaves a natural, slightly waxy look, they can be steamed. It is not a difficult process, but care must be excercised, or you can spoil flowers that may have taken hours to make.

There are really only two things to remember, the first is quite obvious – you will need stems on the flowers, or risk a burn to your fingers. The second thing you need to know is that steaming only works on flowers that have been made with a paste that incorporates Copha *(solidified oil)*. If you use a recipe that does not include Copha, a small amount can be added when you are working up your paste, prior to making the flowers.

Steaming will "set" the colours on chalked flowers beautifully. If you fancy leaves with a heavier shine, then steam them twice, allowing them to dry between treatments.

How do you actually do it? Easy! Simply pass your flowers, one at a time, through a head of steam, about 25cms *(10 ins)* away from the source, then stand them in florist foam to dry. Make sure that they don't touch each other, or they will stick together. Initially they will look just plain wet, but don't panic. Set them aside where they can dry fairly quickly *(so they don't have time to sag)*, and the finished result should be a far more natural looking flower.

There is an alternative to steaming, that of lightly spraying the flowers with spray-on non-stick cooking oil. However, you run the risk of the spray spitting, and also the possibility of dust etc sticking to the finished flowers. It is not as good a method as the steaming.

Creating Lace & Embroidery

I am often asked the question "how do you keep finding new ideas?" The answer is that I am always on the watch for any idea that I can turn to my cake decorating advantage. If you are receptive, there are ideas everywhere. One of my favourite lace designs was inspired by the back of a chair in a MacDonalds Restaurant. I admired it, realised it could be adapted for my use, and copied it on to a napkin. Another lace piece was etched on a glass bathroom door in a movie. As the murderer crept towards the innocent in the shower, I was frantically duplicating the lovely design onto the corner of a newspaper. With a little work, it became a very useful pattern.

The same reasoning applies to embroidery patterns, except that for these I try to get inspiration from the top decoration of a cake. Consider whether the overall concept is for a round feel, or more angular.

Should the border merely compliment the rest of the cake, or be a feature on its own? Generally, the bigger or more spectacular the flowers on a cake, the less it needs to rely on lace and embroidery, and the simpler it should be. Conversely, if you choose a small spray, then the bolder the side border can be – either trough the use of bright colours (and this includes ribbons), or by using big embroidery designs, long extensions, or large lace pieces. To keep a balanced look, all the weight (whether visual or actual) should be towards the base of the cake.

This means that if you are using two different coloured ribbons, then the darker or deeper colour should be towards the bottom, and piping should be heavier or closer together as you work down the side. This is why extension work always looks so good. Not because it requires more expertise to do well, but because it adds visual and actual weight to the base of any cake. Remember however, by flooding a board, you can visually extend the "base" of a cake right to the edge of the cakeboard.

Most people lack only the confidence, not the ability, to design their own embroidery, so I have included in this book what I call my "universal embroidery" pattern. It always starts as one grateful curved line. Then, depending on the cake decoration, I add suitable finishing touches – oak leaves and acorns, pine needles and nuts, holly and berries, or small flowers and leaves. I can turn the pattern either up or down, or lay it on its side. I have taken it to a

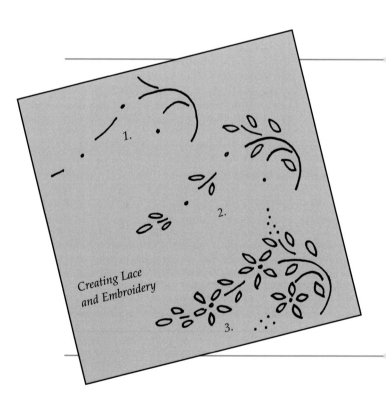

Creating Lace and Embroidery

Top Christmas can be a hectic time for many cake decorators, so any shortcuts are generally appreciated. Using commercially available candy canes makes for a quick, as well as attractive decoration. Although the purist may wish to make their own canes out of icing, experience has shown me that the recipients of the cake usually appreciate the bought ones far more than tasteless icing ones. To make them appear longer, I break them in the centre where they cross over, the gap being hidden by the holly and ribbon bow. To make them even longer, use four canes – two whole ones at the top, then break the hook off another two and use them to extend down from the crossover point. If you live in a very humid climate you may find that the canes will become sticky, so look for the ones that come tightly wrapped in cellophane. I have changed my universal border pattern to incorporate holly and berries for the side decoration, and traced then brush flooded the greeting on the top.

Bottom Fast Old Fashioned Roses form the main adornment on this medium oval engagement cake. Small blue daisies, and two moulded hearts finish it off. The same daisy cutter was used to make the border flowers in three shades of pink, along with blue piped dot flowers. Blue piping for the congratulatory message, and blue ribbons at the base of the cake and around the edge of the flooded board tied it all together.

copying machine and enlarged or decreased it in size, and it looks good in plain white, coloured or flooded. Ribbon goes well with it, and it couldn't be easier to alter or use. To personalise it for your own cakes, start by drawing in the stem line using a fine black marker pen, then use a pencil to add on appropriate leaves, nuts, flowers etc. Anything that doesn't look quite right can be erased, and if you use tracing paper, you can trace in leaves and flowers off other patterns. Once satisfied, decide how many times it is to be traced on to the cake, mark the spaces with a divider, and transfer the pattern you have just created on to the side of your cake. After you have used this pattern a few times you will have gained confidence in your own abilities, and may feel ready to design your own pieces entirely. Just follow the same method i.e. draw a line that represents the basic shape you are after, then fill it in with stems, leaves, flowers or whatever. Keep in mind the fact that a pencil line will be finer than actual piping, so don't crowd the design. If you have difficulty getting it just right, try turning it upside down, or on its side – a different perspective often helps you see where mistakes are. Try replacing the original lines with dots, leaves, a row of flowers, or a succession of shorter lines. When you feel you have captured roughly the look you want, go over the design with a permanent marker, and then continue using the pencil to embellish it, erasing and altering mistakes until you have exactly what you want. You will be surprised to find Just how easy designing patterns is, once you give it a try.

Extra height and importance was added to this two tier hexagonal cake by lifting the flowers for the top tier on to a stand. On both tiers the stands were edged in a continuous piece of cutter lace. The sprays consist of cream Singapore orchids, and tiny yellow orchids with a few Bellflowers (white with a dusting of pink in their centres), and plenty of leaves and ribbon loops. The Chantilly Lace border was designed to match with an orchid motif, and held in place by extending the pattern on to the cake itself. The flooded boards were finished with a matching satin ribbon. The cakes were 10" and 6", and the sprays were arranged on edible discs for easy removal.

Chantilly Lace Border

If you love the effect of extension work, but dispair of ever achieving it, then a Chantilly Lace Border may be your answer. It has a similar effect on the side of a cake as extension, but is relatively easy to make and attach. The biggest hurdle is in designing pieces of the correct size and shape to fit your cake. However, once you have designed a suitable piece, then the template can be retained and reused – often with only minor adjustments.

Attaching pieces of decorated tulle to cakes is not new. In the past, the pieces were stiffened into shapes, embroidery piped on, then attached – not quite achieving the look of true lace. Chantilly Borders differ in two ways: Firstly, the patterns are flooded directly onto the tulle, so as with real lace, it will be made of tiny squares, each one forming a part of the pattern. Secondly, the pieces are made flat, then gently curved into shape before attaching. In order to do this, it is important not to have a continuous or unbroken pattern – there has to be spaces where the tulle can bend. If you observe this principle, then the lace is surprisingly flexible as well as strong. If designed properly, a piece will easily curve enough to go round a central pillar on a tiered cake.

Depending on the size of the pieces of lace you design, the tulle may have to be quite stiff, yet still have very fine holes. I have found that the circles and squares produced for use as "Bomboniere" make the best lace. When buying pieces, try to select styles that have as little pattern, and as much usable tulle as possible.

Because designing pieces is easiest for square sided tins, the following pattern and instructions are for a medium hexagonal cake. (*As tins vary somewhat in size, check a pattern piece against the side of your ICED cake, before starting, and adjust it if necessary*).

Step 1 (*see diagram*). First measure the side of your ICED cake, then add approximately 1cm (*more if you want it to extend further out from the cake*). Draw a line on a piece of paper to the chosen length, and keep your design within it.

Step 2 Now draw an upward curved line from end to end.

Step 3 Draw a curve below the line and to about half the depth of the top line.

Step 4 Cut this out, and hold it against the cake. Pull the ends inwards, rest the top curve against the cake, and the base should flare out, just as normal extension would. You may have to trim off or add to the bottom to get it just right.

With the shape decided, draw on your lace pattern - try looking at real lace for inspiration. You could have a nursery design for christening and children's cakes, feature a ring or hearts for an engagement cake, two rings, bells or doves for a wedding cake, and keys for a 21st cake. You may even take the design off an invitation for a co-ordinated approach.

If you plan to finish off with conventional lace pieces above your Chantilly Lace, then keep the design away from the top border, to avoid a cluttered effect.

Once having designed the lace, the rest is fairly simple. Place the pattern on a flat surface, and cover it with greaseproof paper, or better yet, freezer plastic. Lay a piece of fine nylon tulle over the plastic, secure it in place so it can't slip, and with a paint brush and flood consistency royal icing, paint on the pattern. Alternately, you can put the same thin icing into a bag and use a fine tube to fill in the

design. Use either white or tinted icing, or wait until it has dried and gently chalk on colours. A little Silver Snowflake powder mixed with water, and painted over the finished dried pattern, will give a satin lace effect. Once thoroughly dry, use a sharp scalpel to cut out the whole pattern shape, then carefully lift it off the plastic.

Because the pattern, plastic, and tulle need to be held firmly in place while you work, a hint on how to achieve it may be in order. I purchased an 8 inch *(21cm)* embroidery hoop, removed the inner ring, and replaced it with a solid circle of craftwood of a matching size. Lay your pieces of pattern etc on the flat surface of the centre round, and secure it in place with the outer ring. *(This piece of equipment is handy for any loose pieces of floodwork.)* I have found that the Bombonierie circles with the flocked borders allow for better grip by the outer hoop, and so keep the tulle beautifully tight and flat.

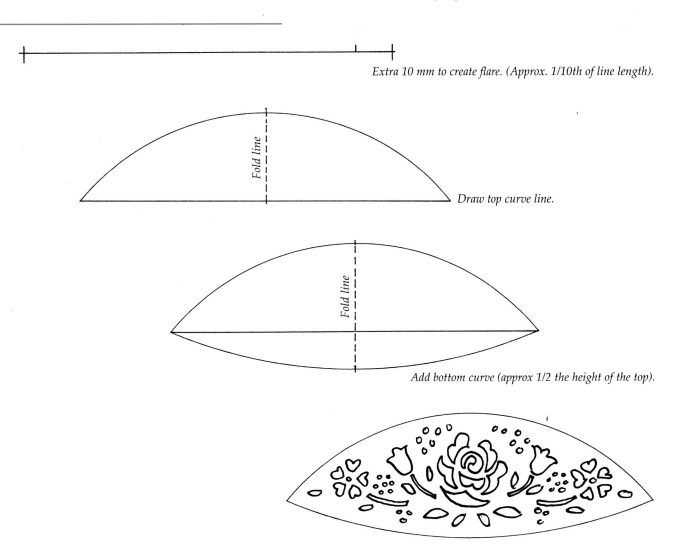

Extra 10 mm to create flare. (Approx. 1/10th of line length).

Fold line

Draw top curve line.

Fold line

Add bottom curve (approx 1/2 the height of the top).

Add appropriate design.

To attach the lace pieces, simply pin the two ends in place on the cake, then use more pins to keep the top in place. Pipe a few dots of icing to hold it permanently, and remove the pins once they have dried. Make sure the pins only go in just far enough to hold the lace, and avoid leaving big holes that will be hard to camouflage later. You can finish off by attaching conventional lace, or pipe dots or snail trail along the top. One of the easiest and neatest trims is piped dot lace. For a really elegant finish, continue flooding the lace design up on to the sides of the cake. Whatever you choose, make sure it helps to hold the lace in place, for despite its delicate appearance, Chantilly Lace Borders that have been properly secured are surprisingly strong. Cakes that have to be transported long distances are excellent candidates for a Chantilly lace Border.

Tiered Cakes

Designing pieces of lace for tiered cakes is a little more complicated, but by making use of modern copying equipment the job becomes a breeze. If you continue to add just the the same amount of flare to to each sized piece of lace, they will stick out progressively further on each tier. By the time you arrive at the third or fourth tier, they would be completely out of proportion. It therefor follows that the extra you allow for flare should be a proportion of the size of the lace. If, for instance, the lace on the base tier is to be 10cms long, and you add an extra centimetre to help it flare out, then you have added one tenth extra. If the gaps between pieces on the middle tier are at 7cm intervals, then the pieces of lace should be 7.7 cms i.e. one tenth bigger. Most modern copying machines can be programmed to enlarge drawings to any size you stipulate, so it is an easy matter to have the initial pieces reduced or increased to suit the dimensions you require. Just remember that the SPACES within a pattern will also become bigger or smaller, and make provision when creating the initial design.

While an unusual combination of shapes, this cake still manages to convey a sense of tradition and romance. The base cake is a large oval on a flooded board. The length of the extension work was visually extended by not only having the lace lie flush against it, but by placing it so that the flooded portion would hide the top line of it. It was also done this way to stay in keeping with the simplicity and clean lines of the top tiers, the second of which is a teardrop. In order that this tier should exactly follow the lines of the base cake, I simply cut a small piece out of the front of a medium oval to form the teardrop shape. When levelling this cake, I also cut it to the height of the top tier (2"), as the hidden board beneath it gives added height. The ribbon (24cm) went round the cake after it was put in place, to help hide a tiny gap caused by slightly uneven covering on the base cake. The ribbon join is behind the arrangement of mauve edged Lisianthus, Mock Agapanthus (dipped pink) and sprays of tiny yellow-centred blue daisies. The chalked and steamed rose leaves are an integral part of the spray, as are the two loops and one short tail of the wide edging ribbon. There is also an abundance of narrow 1cm ribbon loops. The flowers and candles are all on an edible disc. The four inch top tier (cooked in a tuna tin) is supported by 1/4" clear pillars 2-1/2" (65cms) tall. The ribbon around this cake is 16cm wide, while the spray of flowers which completely covers the top was also made on a disc. Bridal white ribbon finished the board edges of both the top and bottom tiers.

Designing Cakes

All cakes and their floral decorations should be designed - that is, you should have a thought out plan of how your cake(s) will relate to each other, and the space they will occupy. *(The spaces you create are just as important as the decorations themselves)*. Normally, you start with the cake, the outline or shape of which will influence the entire creation, whether blatantly or subtly.

While there are no strict rules, generally speaking, rounded cakes tend to look less formal than those with straight sides. Or put differently, straight lines tend to be more masculine than curved lines.

Whether you are aiming for a feeling of grandeur, a sense of peace or excitement, or a masculine or feminine look, your aim should be the same when designing a cake. That is, that the viewers eyes should be gently drawn towards the main feature, rest a moment, then move on to other components, without any feeling of disturbance. The same principles of design that you use in creating a cake can be applied to the floral arrangements and embroidery. While not every cake or its decorations can include all of the following principles, most should include some, otherwise there would be no design, only chaos.

HARMONY   There should be unity within any arrangement, whether you are viewing a group of cakes, or a floral spray. When viewed, neither should present any jarring notes, or feelings of disturbance, or create a sense of "something is missing". If your creation evokes any of these feelings, then check the following principles to see where you may have gone wrong, and how you can correct the problem.

TRANSITION   Transition relates to the element between two objects of different size, shape, or colour. Just as on a stacked wedding cake we include an eight inch cake between a ten and a six, so floral arrangements need intermediate sized flowers between very large and very small ones. This transition also applies to colour. For example, on a spray of bright red roses and white Gypsophila, using medium sized flowers in a deep complimentary colour, *(violets)*, or white tipped with a touch of red *(spray carnations)*, would create transition. It can also be achieved by using gradual colour changes – shading from dark to light colour.

GROUPING   It can be far more effective to group flowers than simply spot them through an arrangement. Grouping can be by colour, shape, or size, and it can also create lines within the basic shape of an arrangement. When you see a three tiered cake where the centre cake sits flush on the base cake or has short pillars, and the top tier is raised on much taller pillars, then you should recognise it as grouping.

CONTRAST   While harmony is important, contrast creates interest and excitement. It can be achieved by a change in colour, shape, size or texture. Colour and size contrast are both fairly obvious elements. For shape, think of a petal cake with a bell top tier, or an oval base with a teardrop top. Think also of the roundness of a rose, compared with the pointed petals of an Agapanthus. Because an entire cake is based on the same medium *(that of icing)*, then contrast, or change of texture can be very important. Textural change can be introduced by glazing leaves, painting on a pearl effect, the including of ribbons or the addition of artificial aids, such as rings or ornaments. Even the use of stamens, or pollen in the centre of a flower creates a change in texture.

Designing Cakes
Continued

REPETITION This means the continual use of a particular line, colour, texture or theme. Consider the same ribbon around the sides of the cake as used in the spray. Repeating a flower colour in any greetings, names or embroidery piped on the cake. Both are examples of repetition. If you have a round arrangement on a cake, and include embroidery in a round configuration, that also constitutes repetition, as would using gold rings and a gold board trim together on a cake.

BALANCE Balance is very important, and it can be real or visual. In a spray, balance is achieved by having the largest and or brightest flowers in the centre. On a cake, it is having a border with the thickest, or what looks to be the heaviest part, at the bottom. Or the widest or deepest coloured ribbon around the base, or even on the board edge. It means having the largest and brightest spray on the bottom cake in a group or tier, and not on the top one. Balance is having the cake sitting on a board that does not overwhelm it with size or colour, or a board that looks inadequate. If everything is in balance in size, colour, shape and form, then you will have come full circle, back to the first element of good design – you will have harmony!

Acorns

Acorns, among other nuts and berries, can be included on the list of decorations deemed suitable for masculine cakes. They are easy to make and arrange, and in the form described below, represent the generally accepted concept of an acorn.

Tape short lengths of 26g wire brown, and fold the tip back down its length, to provide better grip when inserted in the paste.

Tint a quantity of icing brown, using either paste colour, or powder *(see page 10 for hints on making dark colours)*. I have added a touch of red to make tan, rather than plain dark brown. Pinch off a small piece of paste, and roll it into a ball, making sure it has a smooth, crease-free finish. Moisten the folded tip of a wire stem and insert it into the paste. Lay the ball and stem in the palm of your hand, and with the middle finger of your other hand, gently roll the ball back and forth until it has become elongated *(see photo top right)*. Sit in florist foam and leave to thoroughly dry.

Once dry, prepare some edible shine *(see page 94)* and dip each nut into it. Twirl them thoroughly, so that you don't have excessive amounts of glaze running down the stems. Replace the nuts in the foam.

When the shine has set, colour a small amount of royal icing brown *(omit the red colouring)* and using a small tube - I suggest an O-pipe tiny dots over the base of the acorn to roughly half way up. Try to keep the dots small and irregularly arranged. Set aside to dry.

Cutters for the Oak leaves are freely available. I use both GEM and ORCHARD, often mixed together to provide variety. Remember to colour co-ordinate the leaf stems with those of the acorns. You can colour the leaves green, but they are equally attractive in Autumn tones. Arrange them in sprays that will suit the shape of your cake. I like to add a ribbon bow for colour, and a change of texture.

This very simple cake relies as much on the border design as it does on the top decoration for its impact. Although only a medium oval, the flooded board tends to make it seem like a much bigger cake. The side ribbons are in two shades of brown to echo the colours of the acorns. Gold writing and board trimming enhance the cream of the basic covering.

Cotoneaster

If you are looking for a very quick and easy arrangement for a cake, a stem of Cotoneaster can't be beaten. After a spring show of very small rose-like flowers, the trees produce masses of colourful berries against a background of new, dark green shiny leaves. There are several varieties of Cotoneaster, with different coloured berries on each – purple, lacquer-red *(suitable for Christmas cakes)*, yellow/orange, and black. I have used white paste with ample amounts of solidified oil worked in, then dipped and steamed the finished berries for a natural waxy look. However, if you are really rushed for time, you could start with coloured paste.

Begin by covering lengths of fine 30g wire with brown parafilm tape, pulling it almost to breaking point, so that the finished stems are still very thin. Cut the wire into approx 2" *(5cms)* lengths, and bend just the very tip over onto itself, for better grip.

Colour a small amount of paste dark brown or black, roll it until very thin, then cut out one tiny blossom for each berry. Keep them covered until ready for use.

Work an ample amount of solidified oil into some moulding paste, then pinch off enough to make a pea sized ball. Roll the paste between your hands until it is very smooth, with no cracks, and slightly oval shaped. Dip the folded end of a wire stem into your choice of "glue", and insert the wire into the berry lengthwise. Pull

it through until the folded end disappears into the berry. Moisten the area around the hole the wire has left, and use the damp brush to pick up one of the tiny brown blossom pieces, and put it in place over the wire hole. With a fine pointed tool push the centre of the blossom into the berry, then use the

Top *A simple spray of Cotoneaster berries and leaves trimmed with a pink ribbon, graces this off-white cake for Valerie. A very basic extension border, topped with lace adds a feminine touch. The lace was piped in the off white, then the colour painted on to the spots using a fine brush and the same dipping solution as was used for the berries in the spray. (It is important to let the lace thoroughly dry before painting on the spots or "bleeding" will occur). "Valerie" was traced on then brush flooded, and I chose a matching purple ribbon to trim the board.*

Bottom *A stem of bright orange Cotoneaster berries adorns this cream medium hexagonal birthday cake. The spray contains only 25 berries, so it was quick to produce. The border design was traced onto the cake, then piped and flooded. The name was traced and brush flooded in brown, then touched up with gold to compliment the trim on the flooded board.*

back of a scalpel to press into each tiny petal, at the same time making little creases which extend out beyond the brown paste.

By the time you have done this, the berry should have been pushed into a round shape, rather than the oval you started with. Stand the berry into foam to dry. Once dry, for orange berries, chalk on a deep blush of colour – either on the base, around the stem, or on the side. Dip the berries in a lighter shade of alcohol based colour, allow to dry, then lightly steam. For red berries use straight colour, then steam. For purple, dip in straight colour, dry, then use white powdered chalk to brush on a finishing bloom. To arrange them on the stem, tape two together, leaving about half an inch of stem on each, then tape these pairs of berries into clumps.

Cotoneaster Leaves

Work solidified oil into some moulding paste, add a little green colour, and roll out until very thin. Cotoneaster leaves vary greatly in size at the time berries appear on the bushes, so to achieve the required look, simply cut them out freehand using a sharp scalpel. Work the edges until they are very fine, then add veins. Fold the leaf in half lengthwise, then partially open it and set aside to dry. Melt a small amount of left-over paste, and dip short lengths of 30g wire, taped to match the berry stems, into the paste, and attach to the backs of the leaves. Once completely dry, dip the leaves in a darker green mix of alcohol and colour, and after drying, steam to add a sheen.

The finished leaves of random sizes should be taped into rosettes, then in turn, taped to the main stem, onto which the bunches of berries are added.

Mushrooms & Toadstools

Whilst the last thing a good cake decorator wants is any kind of fungi *in* a cake, there is no reason why they can't become an attractive feature *on* a cake – provided of course they are made of icing. As they come in so many interesting shapes and colours, it seems remiss not to take advantage of the opportunities they offer, especially for men's cakes. The following method will work equally well for Toadstools or Mushrooms, it is simply a matter of choosing the shape that most appeals to you, and will best suit the cake you have baked. Purely as a guide, I suggest Toadstools on oval style cakes, and Mushrooms on round shapes *(including hexagonal and octagonal)*.

To make the job easier, always use very firm paste. It takes quite a bit of paste to form a crop of fungus, so it can be worthwhile making up a special batch *(or half batch)* for the job. I simply add about 1/2 tsp more gelatine and approximately 1 to 2 ozs extra icing sugar to my normal recipe.

Start by working plenty of copha or solidified oil into some firm white or cream paste. Roll the paste into a nice smooth ball before forming it into the shape you require *(flat saucer shape for a Mushroom or tall and narrow for a Toadstool)*. Observation of fungus in my garden and at the greengrocers has shown me that they are rarely perfectly symmetrical, so don't worry about making your basic shape too even. When you are satisfied with the shape, lay it upside down in the palm of your hand, and use the blunt end of a pen or pencil to press into the centre where the stalk would be. Next, carefully work the edges with your fingers, pulling them out just a little, and making them very fine and somewhat uneven. This will represent the skin that initially covers the gills, but which tears away after they have emerged from the ground. Keep the fungus in the palm of your hand, and with a clean sharp scalpel, cut the gills. For realistic looking gills you need to use a cutting action, pulling the scalpel from the centre, out to the edges. Simply pressing into the paste won't achieve

This toadstool cake for Allan relies on colour for its impact. I used a medium oval and covered it in cream icing so that it was less stark, and after placing the toadstools, gave them added importance by surrounding them with chocolate sprinkles. Notice that the red of the toadstool caps is repeated in some of the leaves, which helps to draw the arrangement together. The border design was traced on then brush flooded, with the white spots added last, using an "0" tube and fairly thin icing so that they stayed spots, and not "prickles". The name Allan was traced and brush flooded in the same slightly "off" colour as the base ribbon and the board trim.

a natural effect. You may find it useful to initially mark 8 evenly spaced gills, which you can follow round to help keep them all radiating evenly away from the centre. When the gills are done, push the pencil or pen that you used for marking the centre into a piece of foam, and fit the Mushroom or Toadstool on it to dry. If you have used a good strong paste, it should dry with little or no distortion.

Once the caps are dry you can form the stalks. If you are going to arrange your fungus into a clump or group, then it is best to have all the stems close together at their bases. Therefore you will have to slightly curve or lean some of the stalks, so be sure that you also angle the bases to allow them to sit flat on the cake. At the same time, keep checking that the tops will fit into the hole in the centre of the dried cap, while making the bases a little thicker. For more interest, make all the stalks different in height as well as thickness, and vary the angle at which they stand - again using the dried caps to see if they will all sit the way you want. When you are satisfied, push a length of spaghetti up the centre of the stalk, leaving enough protruding from the end to allow you to stand them in oasis to dry. The spaghetti will also make handling the finished fungus, and attachment to the cake much easier.

While the stalks are drying, choose a colour and paint the gills, using a mix of strong alcohol and either paste or liquid colour. After the gills have dried, chalk or paint the tops, then the stalks when they too have dried. Finally, melt a small amount of moulding paste *(see page 10)*, and use it to securely glue the caps and stems together. In order that the finished fungi will sit comfortably in a group, I arrange the stalks in oasis in the same configuration that I want them on the cake, and then attach the caps. That way you can tilt or angle them to accommodate each other, and still look like a natural clump. Finally, when they are completely set, and you are satisfied with the colouring, they can be steamed. Hold them by the spaghetti ends to avoid blotching the surfaces, and return them to the oasis to dry. Initially, they will look unnaturally shiny, but in a few hours will revert to a more natural appearance.

Spots and Speckles

For small speckles on your fungi, *(and before you have steamed them)* prick a few pinholes in a piece of stiff paper, then sprinkle chalk or petal dust over them. Hold the paper above the Mushroom or Toadstool cap, and tap the paper. Keep tapping and moving the paper until you have the amount of colouring you want. If you are unhappy with the speckles, you can blow them off and start again *(the final spotting will hide any slight residual colour that may remain)*. Gently steam the entire mushroom to set the

speckles, handling it by the spaghetti stem to avoid spoiling the finish. Return to the oasis for a final drying.

For larger spots, make tiny balls of paste, and with a little moisture, stick them in place on the cap. Give them time to firm, then dip or paint the cap with alcohol colour mix. Wait a few minutes, then scrape off the icing pieces. Alternately, if you have a good light, paint on the spots with melted copha (or substitute). Refrigerate for a few minutes, then dip and carefully spin your mushroom. You may have to use a dry brush to wipe off any surplus colour that remains on the spots. If you are planning to dip your toadstools then after forming the cap, moisten a piece of spaghetti, and insert it through the centre to act as a stem when you dip and spin it. The spaghetti is simply snapped off before gluing on the final stem. Dipped toadstools and mushrooms generally don't need to be steamed.

I have incorporated Autumn leaves with the mushrooms on this 9 inch, cream octagonal cake. With the principles of good design in mind, the red on the mushrooms was repeated on some of the leaves, and around the cake base. "Peter" was traced on, then brushed flooded. The order of work on the border design after tracing was to first flood the longest stem, (which is furthest away), then the other stems, making the stem of the largest (and closest) mushroom, thicker. With an "O" tube, and dark brown royal icing, pipe a line under the caps of the two largest mushrooms. Over-pipe three more lines, each one a little shorter than the last, then finish with a fifth line from edge to edge. At this stage the piping should look like a tiny rounded extension border piece. Brush flood on all the mushroom caps – it may take two coats to properly complete the two larger ones. You will see that the dark brown piping on their undersides will show through the pale caps and add shading. After drying, chalk on a very discreet hint of extra colouring if you wish. Finish the board with matching brown ribbon.

Pine Cones and Needles

P ine cones are a very easy and effective Christmas decoration. The only tool needed is a small pair of pointed, sharp scissors. You will also find the job will be made easier if you use a good firm paste. If you are making a few cones, then it is worthwhile making up a special batch *(or half batch)*. I usually add an extra 1/2 tsp of gelatine and 1 to 2 ozs more icing sugar to my usual recipe, for this type of ornament.

Work some copha or solidified oil into your paste *(white or any pale colour you may have left over)*, then form it into a basic cone shape. Moisten a piece of brown taped 22g or 24g wire, or a piece of spaghetti, and insert it in the wide end, pushing it to about half way down the cone. Hold the wire, and with the cone downward, start cutting little "V" shapes into the icing. Start at the top, and keeping the "V"s close together, complete a full circle around the "stem", then work your way down and around, finishing at

Pine Cones and Needles
Continued

the pointed end. It is purely a matter of choice, but I prefer to slightly flatten the tip of each little "V"shape with my finger, before setting the cones aside to dry. Allow at least 2 days to thoroughly dry, before dipping and spinning them in a strong alcohol colour mix. If you use powder to colour your alcohol brown, then remember to allow time for all the powder to disolve before you start work.

Pine needles are even easier to make than the cones. Cut the tips off some stiff stamens, melt some moulding paste (*green if you have left-overs, but white will do*), and either paint the paste on to the stamens, or dip them directly into it. You may find the need to add a few drops of water to the paste, or rejuvinate it in the microwave to keep it at a usable consistency. Sit the needles in florists' foam to dry, then dip in dark green alcohol solution to colour. Dip them far enough into the colour solution to colour a little of

the bare stamen as well as the icing, and they will be easier to tape on to the stem later.

When they are thoroughly dry, tape one to a piece of fine wire with brown parafilm tape (*I split my tape at least once, so that there will be less bulk when finished*). Continue taping needles on to the wire, spiralling them around as you work downwards. Tape only over the bare stamen, not the icing part of each needle, and cut away the excess stamen as you secure each piece. Leave the excess on the last two or three needles to provide some strength to the stem, and finish by folding the needles outwards.

If you want a snow effect on the cones or needles, dip them part-way into some very thin royal icing, and if you want, sprinkle on some of the excellent edible glitter that is now available. Stand the stem into a piece of foam at the same angle that you intend using it in an arrangement, so that the snow icing can drip at a convincing angle.

Agapanthus

Agapanthus, or "Lily of the Nile" as they are often called, are not only beautiful garden plants, but the individual flowers are favoured by florists for their long lasting qualities when wired into bouquets. As well as white, they come in various shades of blue and mauve, and also in extremely tall and dwarf varieties. Some have slightly frilled edges to their petals, while others are straight. They all have a line of darker colour down the centre of each petal - in the white varieties this is a shiny line of white on a dull white petal. They have six stamens, the same colour as the flower, with brown tips in the blue varieties, and yellow on the whites. There is also another, which looks just like a stamen without a tip. The stamens follow the line of the lowest petal, before curling upwards at their tips. There is no calyx as such, although close examination will reveal that three of the six petals will be just a little wider than the other three. All are slightly curved back.

As usual, I take artistic licence when making my own Agapanthus. As you will see when looking through this book, I often use a cutter with only 5 petals if I feel the finished flower will be more suitable for my arrangement. Whether you use a five or six petal cutter, the directions are the same.

Large Agapanthus

You will need a mould to set your Agapanthus in. I use a Karume Azalia mould, but a holed board or flower stand will produce good results. You may also wish to try using small plastic funnels, which have been cut down a little. I also prefer to make my

flowers white, and then chalk or dip them (*thus colouring the stamen stems at the same time*).

Use five or six stamens, depending on how many petals your flowers will have. Choose those with fine tips, or use blank ones that you can tip yourself once the flower is finished. Cut the stamens to approximately the length of the petals on your cutter, and tape them onto a length of 26g or 28g wire with white tape. (*see page 4 for the correct method*). If you want green stems, you can always overtape them later. Use the back of a knife to curl the ends of the stamens slightly, much as you would for curling ribbon.

Roll out some paste until it is really thin, and cut out one set of petals for each flower. Use your fingers or

This is really a very simple traditional cake, but the component parts have come together so well that the finished product is a really outstanding cake. The sprays echoed the bridesmaids' bouquets of pink Roses, mauve Agapanthus, white spray Carnations, and Gypsophila. Lots of lovely long ribbon loops softened the sprays, the top one of which is perched on a pillar (I broke the base off so that it would push down into the cake). Chantilly lace, topped with simple "dot" lace graced the sides. The pillars are all 3 inch, and the octagonal cakes are 6", 8", and 10". Flooded boards with a ribbon trim finished this simple, uncluttered cake.

a fluting tool to thin the edges nicely, and add a little frilling if desired. Lay the flower face up on a piece of thick soft foam, and drag the tip of your fluting tool along the length of each petal, from the centre, out to the tip. Turn them over, and using a ball tool, press the end of each petal to give it a slightly round and curled back appearance. Turn the petals over once more, and with the ball tall, press firmly in the centre. Use your tweezers turned on their side to slip under the petals, and lift them into the mould where they are to dry. Make sure the petals are all evenly spaced. Take the stamen stem and paint a tiny amound of thin melted moulding paste at the base of the stamens, and a little way down the tape. Push the stem through the centre of the flower so that only the stamens, and none of the tape and wire shows. Tilt the stem slightly so that the stamens are just off-centre, with the curved tips facing into the middle, then set aside to dry. If you are not planning to dip the finished flowers, then thin royal icing can be substituted for the melted moulding paste. When dry, melt some moulding paste, and paint it on to the back of the flower and a short way down the stem, to give the flower a more elongated effect. Once this is sufficiently set, paint a small green calyx at the base of the flower, and set aside to thoroughly dry. As a shortcut, you can also paint on just the green calyx, making it longer than usual, and do away with the extra bit to elongate the flower.

When thoroughly dry, brush some colour *(chalk or petal dust)* down the centre of each petal, then dip in tinted alcohol solution – the stamens will also be coloured of course. If you didn't have dark tips to your stamens, then add them last – if done before you dip the flower the colour often bleeds onto the petals.

Buds

Agapanthus buds are very easy. Roll a small piece of paste into a ball in your hands until it is nice and smooth, then work it into a sausage shape, slightly pointed at each end, and with the widest part about a quarter of the way down its length. Dip a piece of thin taped wire in your choice of glue, and insert it into the bud base. Set aside to dry, and then finish with a small green calyx painted on with melted moulding paste.

Mock Agapanthus

If you look closely at some of the cake photos in this book, you will see that where I have used large "round " flowers as the feature, I generally use Mock Agapanthus with them. Their pointed shape adds contrast, and their protruding stamens soften the overall outline. For these Mock Agapanthus I use daisy cutters, in whatever size I deem suitable for my arrangement. Because they are usually small, the super fine stamens are best, and for really small flowers, I use them blank and tip them myself. As added interest, you can also include a little flared calyx made from a very tiny daisy cutter, or an equally small calyx cutter if you have one.

Cut five or six stamens to approximately the length of the petals on the cutter you are using, and tape them on to a length of 28g or 30g wire. Use white tape which won't add any colour to the centre of the flower - you can overtape with green later if you prefer.

Each tier of this teardrop cake is slightly turned, to create a sprial effect, and make it just a little different. The sprays consist of Watsonias (made in egg-yellow paste, then pink dusted on the edges before steaming), along with Watsonia buds, mauve Bell Flowers, and tiny yellow centred white daisies. The small yellow tipped leaves were made from individual daisy petal cutters, chalked and steamed. The sides feature two rows of flooded lace. The top row is inverted and alternated with the botton row, which is attached on the usual angle. To keep the top row flush with the cake as you go round corners, just put a touch of icing on the four top points of it, as well as behind the flooded portion, and gently press the piece against the cake to crack it, but still keep its shape, so that it looks more like embroidery than lace. Remember, if your are arranging the glass pillars in a "mirror image" effect as I have, the top ones must be directly above the bottom ones (visually at least). The boards are trimmed with satin ribbon, and the sprays are on edible discs.

Roll your paste very thin, and cut out one set of petals for each flower. Finger the edges, and use your fluting tool to roll from side to side on each petal. This not only thins them, but will make them a little wider towards the tips. Lay the petals face up on a piece of soft foam, and drag the tip of your fluting tool down the length of each petal to create a vein. If you are making very small blooms, then use a blunt needle or bodkin. Turn the petals over, and press the tip of each with a ball tool. Turn them face up once more, and press in the centre with a ball tool. Lift the flower by turning your tweezers sideways and slipping them under the petals. Place into a holed board or flower stand. You may need to gently press it again in the centre with the ball tool, but take care not to split it. Paint a small amount of thin melted moulding paste at the base of the stamens and a little way down the tape holding them. Insert the wire stem into the centre of the flower, pulling it down until only the stamens and none of the tape shows. Leave to dry.

When they can be safely handled, roll out a small amount of green paste until it is very thin, and cut out one little calyx for each flower. Finger any rough edges, and roll your fluting tool down the length of each point, from the centre out to the tips. If you do this while the petals are resting on your fingers, they will quite often end up with enough curl, otherwise, lay them on soft foam, and press each tip with a small ball tool. Turn them over, and press in the centre with the ball tool. Moisten either the centre of the calyx, or the back of the flower. Insert the stem into the centre of the calyx and push it up the wire and attach to the base of the flower. Allow a short time for the calyx to stick, melt a little of the same green paste, and paint a little hip at the base of the

calyx. When completely dry, add any chalking, and tip the stamens if they require it.

Buds are made by rolling small pieces of paste into shape, and inserting very fine wire – 30g or 32g – and leaving to dry. Finish with a calyx as for the flower, but making the calyx of the smallest buds curl over the bud, rather than away from it.

Bellflowers

Bellflowers is really just a general term I use to describe some handy little filler flowers. They are representative of a variety of different flowers, just depending on the colour you make them. For instance, if made blue, then they quite closely resemble Bluebells. In bright red, they are remarkably like the flowers of a Flame tree. If you vein down the centre of each petal, you will see how much like Hyacinths they are. Is it any wonder I find them so convenient to have handy?

For most of my Bellflowers I use a daisy cutter, however, a Jasmin cutter, and a Rose calyx cutter of the same size both produce extremely pretty substitutes, should you feel like a change.

The secret to these useful little beauties is to allow them to dry for a while in an alfoil shape pressed out of the smallest of the Wilton 2-piece Lily Nails. Fifteen or so of these shapes will be enough, as the flowers only need to sit in them for a short time, after which they can be removed, and will still retain their shape, leaving the mould free to form another flower in. Rest the foil cups in the holes of a flower stand or holed board.

To make the flowers, roll your paste very thin, and cut out the shapes. Cover those you are not working on, and lay the first one on your fingers. In order to make the petals very fine, and encourage them to curl, roll your fluting tool along each petal, from the inside out to the tip, but avoiding the very centre. Work each petal, then lay it on a piece of soft foam. Use a small pin-head size ball tool to press just the tip of each petal, *(to curl it up)*, then turn the flower over, and press it quite firmly in the centre with a slightly larger ball tool. Pick the flower up, and place it over one of the foil cups. With the larger of the ball tools, press the flower down into the cup. Don't just push it in the centre, as unless you are very lucky, it will split. Instead, ease the paste down by pushing it from the sides, pressing in 2 or 3 places until you have coaxed it into shape. Once it is well into the mould, then you can give it a final press in the centre with the ball tool. Give the paste a few minutes to set *(weather dependent usually)*, then remove the flower, insert your choice of stamen and set it into a holed board or flower stand to dry

As for stamens, it depends on the look you want your finished flowers to take. Basically you can insert a single large stamen, or tape several very fine ones to a piece of thin wire *(30g)*, paint the top of the wire *(where it meets the stamens)* with melted moulding paste, and insert it into the flower. Pull it

down, so that only the stamens, and none of the tape shows. If you plan to dip the flowers, it is important to use melted moulding paste, but if not, then thin royal icing will do. Once dry, paint a small green calyx on the back – either with melted moulding paste or thin royal icing. If you dip these flowers, then any stamens will also be coloured in the dipping process.

Bellflowers
Continued

To put yellow tips back on them *(or any colour you desire)*, cut them all off to the same length. Paint just the tips with a brush dipped in thick Tylose glue, then dip the tips into a shallow container of scraped chalk, or petal dust. Just another hint – if you are planning to dip your Bellflowers a dark colour, then it pays to do it before you add the calyx, or it won't be green. Instead, paint a tiny amount of thin white melted moulding paste at the back of the flower to hold it firmly during the dipping process, then add the green calyx last when the flower has dried.

Top The romance inspired by heart shaped cakes keeps them ever popular, and this two tiered double-heart is no exception. Both sprays of pale pink Wirlinga Princess Camelias and small mauve filler flowers are formed on edible discs, so they will be easy to remove for keepsakes. There is embroidery on the tops of both cakes, and in a band above the ribbon insertion on the sides, which were finished with flooded lace. Satin ribbon softens the board edges.

* The wire used in making the Camelias was pulled out of the one or two flowers that went straight onto the cake to create the slight cascade effect.

Bottom A spray of miniature Camellias adorns this large oval engagement cake, which also features a Chantilly Lace border. A diamond ring nestles among gold edged ribbon loops, the two tails of which extend out from the spray and end symbolically with matching moulded hearts. I used Silver Snowflake powder mixed with water to paint the hearts, then carefully edged them with gold so they matched the ribbon.

Camellia Wirlinga Princess

The first thing that crossed my mind when I saw this new miniature Camellia was that some horticulturalist had designed it with cake decorators in mind. It was an ideal size, not too complicated, and looked like it had been freshly chalked. I begged a few blooms from a sympathetic nursery owner, and literally rushed home to begin reproducing them in icing. I hope you will find them as simple and satisfying to make as I did.

Firstly, you will need a mould to form them in. I used a Karume Azalia mould initially *(see page 9)*, but have since found that using the holes in a flower stand also works. Whichever your choice, line it first with alfoil.

Next prepare a stem and stamens. I use the super fine Japanese ones – white or cream with yellow tips are very close to the real thing. Cut the stamens to slightly less than half their length, and tape approximately 15 to 20 onto a piece of 26g wire.

Camellia stamens are straight so don't try to bend or flare them out. Like other flowers though, the tips go brown once they have been pollenated, so paint just a touch of caramel brown on some of the tips.

Roll out some white paste until very thin, and cut two large, and one small set of petals for each flower. *(If you only have the large size cutter, cut three, and trim one set down to size with small sharp scissors)*. Starting with the larger set of petals, finger the edges, and work them with your fluting tool, so that they are not only very fine, but have just a hint of frilling. Lay the petals on a piece of thick soft foam, and drag your fluting tool the length of each petal, starting near the centre, and pulling out towards the tip, creating a slight vein. Press in the centre with a small ball tool, then lift the petals and place them in the mould, forcing the centre well down with your ball tool. Work the second large set of petals in the same way as the first. Touch the centre of the first petals with a little glue or egg white, and position the second set over them, making sure that they alternate. Press the two sets together with the small ball tool, and while still holding the tool in the centre, gently push the tip of each of these last three petals inwards, so that they lift up, and finish with a slightly curled back look.

Work the remaining small set of petals in the same way, again using egg white or glue to hold them in place. It is important to position these last petals so they fall in alternate gaps between the previous two sets *(look carefully at the photographs)*.

Paint a small amount of thin white royal icing around the base of the stamens where the tape starts, and insert the stem into the flower, pulling it through until only the stamens, and no tape shows *(to this end it is better to use white tape, as you can*

The request for a cake with a "baroque" look was the catalyst for this three tiered, off-white, round cake. The sprays featured Lilies, pale peach Rose buds, Eriostemon and some smaller filler flowers, along with plenty of leaves and ribbon loops. They were all made on edible discs. I used two Lilies on each cake, but varied the number of roses and filler flowers. The single cherub, as well as both stands, were edged with a scallop made with a "continuous scallop cutter", and using covering fondant. As the bride's gown featured pearls, the Chantilly Lace border was edged in snail trail painted with a mix of water and Silver snowflake petal dust. I used eight pieces of lace for the two bottom cakes and only seven on the top, as eight would have made the pattern disproportionately small. Finally, the boards were edged with off-white ribbon.

always over-tape with green when the flower is finished). Set aside to dry.

When copying these Camellias, I noticed that about one in four flowers had splits in the narrower petals that then curled or twisted. Some flowers had only one split in one petal, while others had one or more splits going off all three. Apparently it is quite normal, and I found it rather attractive. If you would like this same effect, simply use sharp scissors to cut a narrow strip off the side of the petal, but leave it attached in the centre. Work the petals as before, but when you lay them on the foam use a very small ball tool *(glass pinhead size)* and drag it firmly from the tip of the split, in towards the centre, causing it to twist or curl. Try splitting one petal down the centre, then curl the two pieces and cross them over each other. A few of these different blooms mixed in with some perfect ones gives a far more natural look to an arrangement.

Once dry, there is the calyx to add. You can make a simple, strong, and effective calyx by painting thin green royal icing or melted moulding paste on to the back. For a more detailed one, roll a small amount of green paste until it is very thin, and cut out one calyx for each flower. Finger the edges – they must be very fine to look realistic – lay the calyx on thick soft foam, and press it in the centre with a small ball tool. Paint it with glue or egg white, then slide it up the wire stem and attach to the back of the flower.

To complete your Wirlinga Princess you need to add just a hint of pink on the edges of each petal. To do this, use a soft flat brush, and holding the flower upside down over your container of chalk or petal dust, drag the side of the loaded brush against the petal edges. Any excess chalk will fall away from the flower, so that only those parts that are touched by the brush will be pink. Of course, though this flower is naturally white with pink, there is no reason why you can't make it in any colour you choose. As a finishing touch, steam the completed flowers and leave them for a final drying period.

The leaves are the same dark shiny green as any other Camellia, but proportionately smaller.

Lilies

The instructions below can be used to make almost any lily, with any different cutters, not just the ones I choose to use. You will notice that the stamens are somewhat different to those that are normally associated with lilies, and there is a reason. The stamens on lilies hold a lot of bright pollen, which freely falls off, and which stains. Because of this, a good florist will cut off the tips, leaving just the blank ends, though they sometimes still have a little colouring.

As the lilies on my cakes are usually meant to be copies of those carried by brides, it makes sense to have straight stamens with just a dash of colour *(to keep them from being boring)*, so that they will match the bride's bouquet.

Apart from the cutters, I also use small plastic funnels in which to form the flowers. Mine measure 1-1/2 inches *(4 cms)* across the top and 2-1/2 inches *(6 cms)* from top to bottom. If you are unable to obtain a small funnel, there are lily moulds available.

Prepare the stamens first, by cutting off both ends of six or seven. Paint some glue a little way along one end of each, and dip them in scraped chalk or petal dust. Give them time to dry before taping them on to a short length of wire *(24g or 22g)*, using white tape.

Roll some paste very thin, and cut three each of both size petals. Finger the edges of the first narrow petal *(cover those you are not working on)*. Use a fluting tool to work around the edges, making them very fine, and adding just a little ruffling. Lay the petal on soft foam, and drag your fluting tool down the centre of it. Work the other two narrow ones in the same way, then fit all three into one of the funnels, or a mould. Make sure the ends of the petals are well down into the neck of the funnel, and gently curl the tips back.

Work the three remaining wide petals in the same way. Paint some glue on the petals in the funnel, then lay the next three over them - alternating them of course - and making sure that the tips go well into the funnel, and all are pressed firmly together. Melt some moulding paste, and paint it around the base of the stamens. While you don't want a bulge of paste welling up into the flower, make sure there is enough to help hold everything together. Insert the stamens into the lily, pulling them down until just

the stamens, and none of the tape and wire shows. If any of the melted paste does push up into the centre, use a damp brush to smooth it out. Set aside to dry in the mould or funnel, but once it is firm enough to gently handle, remove it and give the thick area at the neck of the lily time to thoroughly dry. lastly, melt some moulding paste, and paint around the base of the flowers and a little way down the stem to neaten it and add some strength.

Chalk and steam on any colour or highlights you require. Most lilies have a little natural sparkle when viewed in a good light, so brush on just a touch of Hi Liter and potato flour mix before steaming, and they will be just that little more realistic.

Lisianthus

Looking rather like a full blown rose, Lisianthus *(or Eustoma or Prairie Gentian)* belie their delicate appearance. Being so hardy has made them increasingly popular with florists for bridal bouquets, so mastering them will prove beneficial to any busy decorator. Their colours range from white, white with mauve, pink or deep purple edges, to solid pink, mauve and deep purple. The white flowers usually have a green centre, while the brighter colours have a much deeper colour in the centre, giving them a quite dramatic look. They have been hybridised, so colour variations as well as double and triple blooms are available. All of which leaves an imaginative cake decorator plenty of room to be creative.

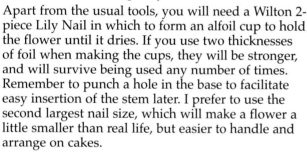

Apart from the usual tools, you will need a Wilton 2-piece Lily Nail in which to form an alfoil cup to hold the flower until it dries. If you use two thicknesses of foil when making the cups, they will be stronger, and will survive being used any number of times. Remember to punch a hole in the base to facilitate easy insertion of the stem later. I prefer to use the second largest nail size, which will make a flower a little smaller than real life, but easier to handle and arrange on cakes.

To make the pistil take two small pieces of paste *(pale green for white flowers, dark, almost black for deep colours)*, and work them into two tiny "carrot" shapes. Press the two shapes together, and roll them between your two index fingers just down from the thick end, so the tops spread out a little. *(As you look down on the pistil it should look like two little round balls side by side)*. Insert a strong wire

(22g – 24g) into the paste just below the two little round parts, and work the paste over and down the wire a short way - about 1/2 an inch. Pinch off any excess, and set aside to dry. When dry, paint them the desired colour if you didn't colour your paste,

and glaze them, as they should have a fairly glossy finish.

Select 5 large round headed stamen, paint them with a little tylose glue *(or egg white)* then dip them in bright yellow chalk or petal dust. Leave to dry. Once both the pistil and stamens are dry, tape the 5 stamens around the pistil. Initially, the stamens should be just a little higher than the pistil, but once taped, use your tweezers to put an "L" bend in them, so they stand away from the pistil, and finish up the same height. Paint the stamen stems to match the colour of the centre of the flower *(alcohol mixed with liquid colour and brushed on, is the easiest way to do it)*.

Because of the stamens and pistil, these flowers really can't be dipped, so any colouring must be done as the flower is made. They do however come up well with steaming, so remember to work in some solidified oil as you go.

Lisianthus
Continued

Roll your paste very thin, and cut one set of petals for each flower, *(unless you want a double or triple bloom).* If you want deep colour in the centre of the bloom, or on the petal edges, then dust it on now, and blend it in with your fingertips. Work around each petal with a fluting tool, making it very fine, and adding some movement, but don't make it too frilly. Lay the petals on a piece of thick soft foam, and press in the centre and just a little way up the petals with a large *(marble size at least)* ball tool. Lift the petals, and place them in an alfoil cup - it is best to have the cup still in the nail as you do this. Arrange the petals so they each overlap, and with the end of a brush or your fluting tool, curl the edge of each petal over. *(I find it easiest to do now, but if you have difficulty, try curling the petals back before you put them into the alfoil cup).* If you have chosen to use individual petal cutters, then remember to glue each petal well as you place it in the cup. As you look down into the flowers, those that are not fully open should have a slight spiral effect, so use cotton wool pieces to hold the petals the way you want them. For flowers with a half open look, simply squeeze the top of the alfoil cup in a little, till the flower is the right size. This is your last chance to add colour to the centre of the flower, so if you haven't already done so, brush it on now, as once the stamens and pistil are in place, it will be almost impossible to do.

When you are satisfied with the way the petals are sitting, paint a little melted moulding paste *(the same colour as the centre of the flower)* on to the prepared stem, just below where the stamens are taped. Lift the alfoil cup out of the nail, and insert the stem into the flower, pulling it down so that just the stamens and none of the tape shows. Because of the speed with which melted paste dries, it is best to wait until you have several flowers ready before adding the stems. Support the flowers in a flower stand until dry.

Lisianthus have a calyx much like a rose, but far narrower – almost just a spike of green resting against each petal. I use a normal rose calyx cutter, as it will add strength when glued to each petal, and in most arrangements, won't show anyway. However, if you are striving for realism, then use a pair of curved nail scissors to cut off some paste either side of each point, to achieve the desired look. Again, if you wish to create a botanically correct flower, then the colour of the underside of the flower should correspond with its centre *(green where the centre is green, purple where it is purple etc).* However you choose to make the calyx, the method is the same.

Form a small pea sized ball of green paste, and push it up the wire stem, and with a little glue, attach it to the underside of the flower. Roll out some green paste and cut out 1 calyx for each flower. Finger the edges, and cut away some of the width of each point if you wish. Use your fluting tool to drag down the centre of each point, then lay the calyx on a piece of soft foam and press in the centre with a ball tool. Paint the whole calyx with your choice of glue, then insert the flower stem in the centre of the calyx and slide it up the wire. Mould the calyx over the little piece of green paste, and attach a point to the back of each petal. Again if absolute realism is your aim, pinch the paste at the base of each calyx point *(I use a pair of blunt end tweezers)* so that if you look down the stem at the base of the calyx, it will have a "star" effect. Set aside to dry. Although they don't really have one, I add a very small "hip" of melted green paste, as this gives strength, especially desirable if you will be wiring your finished Lisianthus into a spray or bouquet.

Buds

Lisianthus have beautiful buds, and are worth the effort involved in making them. The petals are pale

Lisianthus
Continued

green, with just a hint of their future colour, and spiralled. Naturally the calyx has the same extremely narrow points as the full flower, which, on small immature buds protrude beyond the petals, and twirl around each other. As the bud grows, the petals gradually overtake the calyx points, and they look more like a slightly elongated Rose bud.

I usually prefer to chalk or petal dust on any colour required, but you can start with pale green paste if you prefer. Work a small amount of solidified oil into your paste, and form four small "fingers", each one tapered at the ends. Hold the four pieces at one end, then twist the tops as you press them together. Smooth them over until they form a long narrow bud with slightly spiralled petals. Moisten the end of a piece of wire that will be strong enough to support the finished bud, and insert it. Set aside to dry. Once dry, colour some paste green *(a slightly blue-green is the correct colour)*, form a small ball of paste, slide it up the wire and attach with glue to the base of the bud. Roll out some more paste very thin, and cut out one calyx for each flower. Use small sharp scissors to trim each point of the calyx until they are no more than very thin spikes, lay on soft foam, and press in the centre with a ball tool. Paint your choice of glue all over the calyx, push the stem of the bud through

the centre, and slide it up the wire and mould it over the little ball of green paste. Press the points against the bud, making sure they are evenly spaced, and if they protrude above the petals, twist them once before flaring them out slightly. Use your thumb and forefinger to pinch the paste at the base of each point, so that the "hip" of the calyx is more star shaped than round. Set aside to dry, then finish with a light dusting of chalk colour. For the astute reader who has noticed that I advocate only four petals on the bud, not five, there is a purpose. For some reason, three or four pieces seem to make the best buds, while five pieces usually produce a bud that looks too fat, and the petals too close together. As I said at the beginning, they are very attractive buds, but if you are pressed for time, a normal Rose bud will be an acceptable substitute.

While this cake was designed for a birthday celebration, with the addition of doves or rings, and the elimination of the name, it would make a very glamorous wedding cake. The cake itself is a large long-octagonal, with a flooded board. The spray consists of white double Lisianthus and buds, mock Agapanthus, and forget-me-nots wired to represent Gypsophila, plus plenty of green leaves and ribbon. The front and back daisy embroidery was flooded to match the lace, and a simple dropped loop border added at the base between the extension work on the short sides.

Shirley Lilies

A cutter lying unused since purchase 10 years earlier, and a search through my book of 1001 flowers gave me the inspiration to create these Shirley Lilies *(Lilium inventious gadorii)*. As you can see, they have somewhat "softer" appearance than the lilies normally used in cake decorating – and they are easier to make!.

As well as the cutter, you will need alfoil cups made from the second largest of the Wilton 2 piece lily nail set. I have veined my

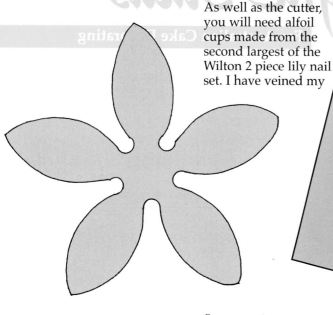

flowers using a Cosmos veiner *(pictured)*, but if you haven't access to one, then use your fluting tool where I use the veiner, as these lilies are still attractive with smooth petals.

Take approximately 12 – 20 very fine whole stamens, and arrange them so they are slightly uneven. Bend a length of white taped 26g wire over the centre of

the stamens, then use pliers to squeeze the two ends of the wire tightly together, holding the stamens securely upright. Avoid twisting the wires, as this results in an ugly stem.

Re-tape the wire, starting right up against the stamens, to help keep them in place. They should spray out nicely so they will fill the centre of the lily.

Roll your paste very thin, and cut two sets of petals for each lily. Cover the ones you are not working on, and finger the edges of the first set. Work around each petal with a fluting tool, not so much to flute them, but to give a little movement, and make them super fine. As they are a little too big to do on your fingers, lay the petals face up on a board, and roll a Cosmos veiner tool backwards and forwards across the length of the petal. Roll from edge to edge first, then make shorter rolls till you finish by simply pressing along the centre. As well as creating veins,

Dusky pink chalked Shirley Lillies, pale apricot Bellflowers, and blue daisies decorate this two tier bell cake. Each spray also features darker pink ribbon loops, and long leaves that were chalked with a touch of pink along the central vein before steaming. The length of the side extension work was visually extended by not only having the lace lie flush against it, but by placing it so that the flooded portion would hide the top line of it. Using the lace in this manner also helped to accentuate the bell shape, as did the ribbon insertion on the top. Flooded boards provide security for the top tier, which is on a 45 degree angled stand. Both sprays are on edible discs, including the angled cake, which I found needed no extra fixing, but was held safely in place by the lugs, and the weight of the spray itself.

it will make the sides of the petal lift up. Lift the petals on to a piece of soft foam, and press in the centre with a large bell tool. Place the petals over an alfoil cup, and use the ball tool to press them right down into it. For a fully open flower, gently fold the petals back. Leave them upright for a half-bud. Work a second set of petals in the same way. Paint a little glue in the centre of the first set of petals, then place the second set over them – alternating the petals. Press down firmly with a ball tool to ensure they are well stuck together.

Paint a little melted moulding paste at the base of the stamens, then insert the stem into the flower, pulling it down so that only the stamens, and no wire or tape shows. Set aside in the alfoil cups to dry thoroughly.

Colour some paste green, and cut out a single calyx for each flower. Finger the edges, then lay them on a piece of soft foam and then press each tip with a small ball tool. Turn the calyx over, and press in the centre before painting it with a little glue. Push the lily stem through the centre of the calyx, and slide it up and attach it to the back of the flower. Melt a little of the green paste, and paint a hip at the base of the calyx, to add strength, as well as a neat finish. Once dry, chalk and steam for the final touch.

The combination of pink Tulips, Singapore orchids and cupids, creates a very romantic look for this four tier hexagonal cake. The sprays are all mounted on edible discs, and include Mock Agapanthus and plenty of ribbon loops to compliment the main flowers. A continuous lace cutter was used to make the trim around the cupid stands and the single top cupid. The sides feature Lily-of-the-valley embroidery, two rows of ribbon and graduated flooded lace. Satin ribbon finishes the boards. Cake sizes are 12", 10", 8" and 6".

Tulips

Now that nurseries have have developed techniques that enables them to guarantee tulip blooms for 9 months of the year, they will feature more prominently in bridal bouquets, and it follows that they will obviously be requested more often for cake decorations. Learning to make them will eventually become a necessity. They are not hard to make, and come in a multitude of colours - from white and yellows to lurid red and orange streaked, from pinks to purples, and even black. Because of their fabulous colour range, they are set to make a quite spectacular contribution to cake decorating.

As I have only been asked to use Tulips on wedding cakes where they are to match the bride's bouquet, and as most florists only use them in bud form, my instructions lean towards making them just so. At this stage of development, the petals are not so much veined, as sort of tightly pleated. As it takes fairly close inspection to reveal these creases, I don't bother with them, although if you wish, an orchid or poppy veiner could be used.

You will need a bell mould to form the tulips in – mine is 1-1/2" tall *(4cms)* and is 1-7/8" *(4.5cms)* wide at the lip. You may find a small wine glass with similar proportions will also work *(after all, many wine glasses are referred to as Tulip shaped).* Line the mould with aluminium foil right up to the lip, so you will have something to get hold of when you want to remove it.

For each Tulip that will be open enough for you to see into, you will need 6 blank stamens. Take a tiny ball of moulding paste and push the tip of a stamen into it. Now roll the paste ball between your thumb and forefinger to form a tiny bulge on the end of the stamen – about 1/4" or half a centimetre long. Make sure both ends of the bulge are tapered, then set aside to dry. Do 5 more. Take another slightly bigger ball of paste and work in some solidified oil, then form it into a pistil similar to those of lillies. Use a mould if you have one, but otherwise it should be shaped rather like a three-leafed clover as you look down on it. Tape a strong wire *(20g or 22g)* with green, tip it with just a touch of glue, and attach the pistil head to it. When the stamens are dry, paint them with glue, and roll them in chalk or petal dust to represent fine pollen. Most Tulips have either yellow or black stamens. When the pistil is dry, dip it in chalk or petal dust, then steam it so it has a waxy look, and the colour is set. For pale coloured Tulips I usually make them green, but many of the deep colours have almost black pistils. Tape the six stamens around the pistil and about half an inch down from it, arranging them so they protrude just a little above it. If your Tulips are to be completely closed, you can do away with the stamens, and simply use a piece of wire with the tip bent at right angles, and a generous dob of melted moulding paste to hold it securely in the base of the flower.

Colour your paste, and work in some solidified oil. Roll it out very thin and cut six petals for each flower. The paste must be really fine at the tip of the petal at least, or the Tulips will look far too heavy. Work the edges of the first petal until they are extremely fine, then lay it on a piece of thick *(at least 2 inches thick)* soft foam. Rub a large ball tool all the way round the edges, and down the centre, pressing very firmly, till the petal looks the right shape. You might like to try using a spoon for this, as the finished shape is much the same. Use your fingers to curl the top sides of the petal in a little, so that it appears a touch more pointed than it really is. Do two more petals the same way, then fit these first three petals into the mould, making sure the points at the bottom only just cross over each other, and are well glued. To pick the petals up, and to control them as I put them in the mould, I lay my fluting tool lengthwise down the centre of the petal, then pick it up with my thumb against the fluting tool, and my middle finger pressed against the back of the petal.

Make three more petals the same as the first. Paint glue on the insides of the first three petals, and if chalking is required in the the centre of the flower do it now, as it is difficult to do well once the flower is finished. Arrange the second three petals in the gaps left by the first three. You will find that in order for them to be level with the others they will need to be overlapped more at the base. Use your ball tool to press the petals firmly against the side of the mould, not only to ensure both sets of petals are well attached to each other, but to make sure the finished flower will have lovely curved sides.

Melt some moulding paste and paint it onto the stem of stamens just below where they are taped in place. Remove the flower from the mould *(still in the alfoil of course)*, and insert the stamens, pulling them well down into the flower. Sit it in a stand or small bottle to dry. If you wish the Tulip to be more open, gently ease the foil back a little. If you wish for a tighter bud, then gently squeeze the foil until the bud is as you want it. Small pieces of rolled foil or cotton wool will help with separating the petals where required. After 12 hours, remove the foil, and leave to finish drying. When dry, melt some green moulding paste, and paint it on around the base of the flower and down on to the stem. Tulips have quite thick stems, and this will not only make yours look more realistic, but will help strengthen it. Chalk and steam the finished flowers as you wish.

To show them to their best advantage, Tulips need to be upright, so try to have some blooms viewed in this position when arranging them in a spray. If they are all laying down and facing forward, it is hard to tell what they are, and all your careful work will be wasted.

Watsonia

If I was asked to describe Watsonias, I would say that they are a dainty version of a Gladioli. Being smaller and more delicate looking makes them ideal for cake decorating. A single, naturally wired stem of buds and flowers lying gracefully across a cake top can look stunning, while single blooms, in company with smaller flowers within a conventional arrangement also have great appeal. Watsonias occur naturally in white, mauve, orange and salmon pink, but of course hybridised colour crosses also exist, so there is room to create your own variations.

Apart from the cutter illustrated, the only special tool you will need is a small plastic funnel – mine measures 1-1/2 inches (4cms) across the top, and 2-1/2 inches (6cms) from top to bottom. I use the funnels as they are, for setting partially opened flowers in, and cut them down to allow for more fully open blooms. They can also be used for setting lillies in, so are a worthwhile addition to any decorators kit.

For each Watsonia you will need four blank stamens, approximately 1-1/2 inches or 3.5 cms long. Take a tiny ball of moulding paste and push the tip of a stamen into it. Now roll the paste ball between your fingers to form a bulge, about 1/4 inch or half a centimeter long, on the end of the stamen. Make sure both ends of the bulge are tapered, then set aside to dry. Do two more. Next dip the tip of the fourth stamen into water, then use your tweezers or your finger nails (if you have strong ones) to pull at the stamen tip and flatten the end. With very small,

very sharp scissors, (and equally sharp eyesight), make 3 downward cuts in the tip of the stamen, and spread these fine little ends outwards. If you can only manage 2 ends, don't worry too much, as even on the real flowers they are extremely fine and difficult to see. As the flowers age, they tend to wither off anyway. Some stamens, once wet, can be unravelled, and you might find this an easier method to try. Once the tips of the first 3 stamens have set, paint the little bulges with your choice of glue, and roll them in chalk or petal dust, to represent fine pollen. Avoid using too much moisture or the pollen will look lumpy and unnatural. Fix all four stamens on to 24g wire with white florists' tape.

Before proceeding further, lightly grease around, and down into the neck of each funnel – a cotton bud does the job quite nicely.

Roll your paste out until it is very thin, and cut six petals for each flower. Work the edges of the first petal so they are smooth and super fine, then lay the petal face up on soft foam. Use a large ball tool to press around the top edge of the petal, so the end is slightly cupped, then pinch just the very tip into a little point. Use a fine fluting tool (such as a curler pin) to press along the length of the stem end of the petal, so that it will fit easily down into the neck of the funnel. Work another two petals in the same way, and sit all three evenly spaced in the funnel.

Work the remaining three petals in a similar fashion, but note that on fully opened flowers, usually one or sometimes all three of these petals can have their tips cupped *back* slightly. They are also just a little larger, so use extra pressure as you finger and work the edges, and their size will usually increase just enough for a natural effect. These petals go in place over and between the first three, and will require gluing. Make sure you press the stem ends of the petals firmly together, or the flower will fall apart when you remove it from the funnel. Again, a curler pin is just right for pushing into the funnel and pressing the petals together.

It is best to wait until you have several flowers made before adding the stamens, as they need to be attached with melted moulding paste (see page 10). Carefully assess the size of the opening left between the petals, and paint enough melted paste around the stamen stem (below the line where the tape meets the stamens), to give the petals something to cling to. However, you don't want dollops of paste bulging up into the centre of the flower, so gauge it carefully. Have a clean damp paint brush handy, so that if it does well up, you can smooth it evenly up the sides of the petals, so that it becomes less obvious.

Set aside for at least 24 hours to dry. There is no air circulating around the base of these flowers, and as

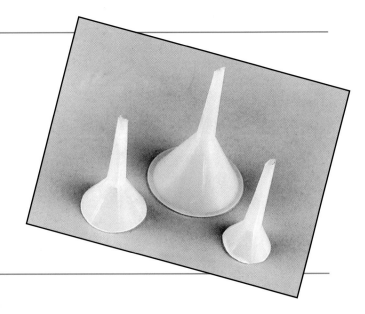

Watsonia
Continued

it is this area that is holding them all together, it is important that it be allowed time to set. Don't presume that the whole flower is dry just because the tips of the petals are. Once the neck area has set, remove them carefully from the funnels, and stand them in foam to finish drying. Often you will find that this same long neck part is either too short, or is not as smooth or even as you would wish, so lengthen it, or touch it up with melted mouding paste. Again, use a clean damp brush to smooth over the joins, and then leave to dry.

Finish off the dry Watsonia by highlighting with chalk colour, and steaming. If you are using them in a conventional arrangement, then finish them off with a calyx painted on with thin green royal icing, or melted moulding paste for extra strength. If you are planning to use them as a natural stem, and are striving for realism, then there is a little added extra

you need to observe. At the base of each flower it has a tiny calyx that consists of two small brown peaks, one each side of the stem. For this I use greaseproof paper that I paint first with food colouring, cut out, then tape into place with pale green florists' tape.

Bright Ideas

For Australian Cake Decorating

A single stem of peach coloured Watsonias accentuates the teardrop shape of this medium size cake. The border consists of overlapping stems of piped and flooded Watsonias above lace and extension work. The board is flooded, and finished with white ribbon overlaid with a 1.5mm wide peach ribbon. Just a tip – when piping any sort of scallops round a teardrop shape, keep them fairly small, or they can create difficulties in the concave area, and around the narrow end.

Watsonia
Continued

Watsonia Buds

As you can observe in the photo, the buds are very basic, just paste rolled onto a piece of 24g wire, and slightly longer and thinner at the bottom than the top *(the widest point should be about one third of the way down the bud)*. Like most buds they are green, fading to colour on the tips. For white Watsonia, first colour the bottom half or so with pale green, then mix a little of the same green with pale pink to brush the tip with. The bigger the bud, the less green and more colour there should be.

This cake epitomises the old adage "less is more". The gold scallop border was cut from a wider piece of lace and carefully trimmed. Watsonias, wired into natural stems decorate the cake tops, and a further two stems held together with a white and gold bow lay beside the stands (chosen for their simplicity). Two gold rings on the base cake compliment the border, as well as the gold edge on the ribbon holding the two stems together. The boards were trimmed with simple white satin ribbon. The round cakes measure 11", 8" and 5".

Zantedeschia

Over the years these elegant lillies have been horticulturally re-named a number of times, the lastest classification being that of Zantedeschia. They have also been Arums, Callas and Richardias. Not only have they suffered frequent name changes, but a lot of bad press as well. In past times, they were frequently associated with funerals *(probably because of their long flowering periods and easy availability)*, and rather unfortunately became known as Death Lillies. Happily, they are enjoying a resurgence in popularity, not only with floral artists, but increasingly with brides. Along with the more common white variety, there is a bright yellow form, as well as pink, and many hybrids in between. For the cake decorator, they are fairly simple to make, and don't as a rule require a lot of filler flowers to accompany them in arrangements.

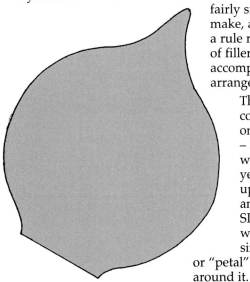

The flower consists of only two parts – a SPADIX, which is the yellow spike up the centre, and the SPATHE, which is the single "leaf" or "petal" that wraps around it.

Cutters for Zantedeschias come in various sizes, it is a matter of you choosing the size you think will best suit your cake. I also prefer to make mine cream, rather than pure white, but there again, it is mostly a matter of personal tastes.

Before starting, have on hand some small pieces of aluminium foil, and as these lillies look best if steamed, work some Copha *(solidified oil)* into your paste.

Colour a small amount of paste a clear yellow, and cover some heavy *(20g)* wire in green tape. Cover the paste and set aside. Colour a larger amount of paste in the colour you have chosen for your lillies, and roll it out until it is fairly thin. Cut out 1 spathe for each flower. Cover the pieces, then work some of the bright yellow paste into a spike, and insert the wire right up into it. Length and width of the spadix will depend on the size of your spathe cutter, but bear in mind that it will appear thicker when you add the finishing touches. Too long is also better than too short. Stand the spadix in foam, while you finger the edges of the spathe, making them as fine

Zantedeschia
Continued

as possible. Lay it either on soft foam, or if you prefer, on the palm of your hand, and run a medium size ball tool all the way way round the curved edges. This will make it easier for you to curl it over later. Turn the spathe over, and paint a little "glue" along the straight bottom edge. Place the spadix length-wise down the centre, and roll the spathe up, pressing quite firmly at the base, and tapering it down the wire. Pinch off any excess paste as you go. At this stage I wrap a small piece of alfoil around the base of the lilly to support it as I slowly open it up, and coax it into shape. Use your fingers to curl the edges over where you want them. Give the pointed tip a twist or curl, but keep in mind that the tip will break easily and may make arranging it awkward later on. When you are satisfied, stand the flower in a holder, or small jar to dry. Remove the foil after a few hours so that the thickest part at the base will also dry properly.

Bright Ideas
For Australian Cake Decorating

Simple wired sprays of lillies, leaves, and ribbon loops make a glamorous statement on this two tier flat-fronted diamond cake. I normally flood my boards by filling a plastic bag with the prepared icing, cut a corner out of it, and pipe the thin icing onto the board. For this cake, I marked a line a little way up the sides, then piped the tinted icing along it, allowing it to run down and on to the board (watch for air bubbles that form right at the base). Once the piece of continuous lace border was attached, the cake had a "floating" look. In keeping with the simplicity of the sprays, the sides were finished with just two rows of ribbon, while two gold rings were added to the bottom tier for interest and balance. Apricot ribbon finished off the board edges.

When the lilly is dry, melt a small amount of green moulding paste and paint it on the base of the flower *(to neaten and strengthen it)*, and take it a short way down the wire *(to represent the very thick stem they naturally have)*.

Of course, everyone has their own ideas on colouring, but for mine, I use a little pale green chalk *(petal dust)* and brush it on the curled tip, as well as in a faint line down the centre of the lilly *(inside and out)*. Add a touch of green up from the stem – the younger the flowers, the more green generally. To finish, I mix a smidgen of pearl dust, or silver snowflake powder with potato flour, and dust all over the lilly, before steaming. When the flower is again dry, paint the spadix with some "glue" *(I use fairly thick Tylose glue for this)* and sprinkle on some Polenta *(also known as maize or cornmeal, and available from health food shops)*.

Zantedeschia Buds

The buds are made in the same way as the flower, but not opened up. Real lillies tend to look as if they are opening near the base and at the top, but are held tight in the centre. A little touch of glue in the middle will help you to get the same appearance. Colouring seems to follow a similar pattern, in that the centre of the bud takes on the colour first, and spreads down to the stem and up to the tip.

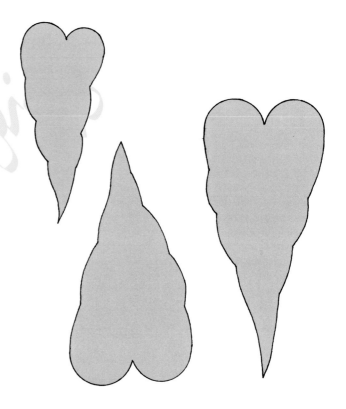

Zantedeschia Leaves

As there are no leaf cutters available in the size and shape that I prefer, I have drawn my own. Most sprays only require between three and five leaves, so making them from a template is no hardship. *(Mine are made from the lid of an ice cream container)*. The three sizes shown will suit the largest of lilly cutters, but if you prefer them a little smaller, then put them through a copier with reducing capabilities.

Colour your paste, and roll it out fairly thin before using the templates to cut out each leaf. I veined mine with a soft rubber poppy veiner, but a Cattleya throat veiner would also suffice. Lightly flute around the edges, but do it so that it goes well into the leaf, not just the very edges. Lay the leaf on soft foam. then drag your fluting tool down the centre from the tip to the stem end. On the smallest leaves, if you press fairly hard, it will fold in half, and the tip will twist or curl, just as the immature leaves sometimes do on real plants. Set the leaves aside to dry, making sure that they are slightly "V" shaped.

Make two or three extra, to give yourself some choice when it comes to arranging them. Melt some of the same coloured paste, dip a piece of taped wire into it, and attach the wire along the vein line at the back of each leaf. When thoroughly dry, either dip them for a rich dark colour, or chalk and steam them.

This very simple, but elegant stacked cake would be an excellent study for a decorator attempting the American style for the first time. The round cakes measure 11", 8" and 5". The border trims consist of a wide off-white ribbon and bow, plus a narrow gold edged base ribbon. Instructions for the vase are on page 76. Although not visible, the small side sprays are repeated on opposite sides of the cake, as is the bow on the centre tier. If you are really pressed for time, a glass or plastic vase filled with fresh or freeze dried flowers would be just as effective. Because the individual cakes were easy to handle there was no need to use raised skewers and holed boards on the top tiers.

American stacked Wedding Cakes

The American style of stacked wedding cakes is becoming increasingly popular. They are not difficult to make, provided you plan carefully before undertaking to make one.

The first point to note comes when cooking the cake - there needs to be at least three inches difference between tiers, so choose shapes that offer the correct sizes. The boards too, are sized differently. The base cake generally needs a fairly large board for balance, and because these cakes are sometimes carried in one piece, it will need to be thicker and stronger than you may be used to using. On subsequent tiers the boards are hidden, so should be the same size as the cake, or only slightly bigger, and the covering icing brought down over it.

As usual, the tiers are supported by skewers, but in this case they are cut to come level with the icing. If you are planning a cake with minimal decoration on the sides *(such as ribbon only)*, and the individual cakes can be handled easily for transportation, then just the supporting skewers will be sufficient.

However, if you are planning on a lot of piping, lace, or even filigree, then the entire cake will have to be transported in one piece, and a little more forward planning is required. Obviously the top tiers must not move, so my solution is to drill two holes *(the same diameter as your skewers)* in the tier boards. Cover the base cake with icing, then gently rest the board for the next tier on it. Mark through the holes with a skewer, then remove the board before positioning the next cake on it, and covering it with icing. Do the same for subsequent tiers. Allow ample time for the covering icing to firm up before proceeding with the next step.

When you are ready to stack the cakes, insert two skewers level with the icing of the base cake, plus two skewers about 1/2 an inch longer, into the two marks that correspond with the holes in the next tier board. Provided all four skewers are evenly spaced, and you fit the protruding skewers into the holes in the tier board as you lower the cake on, it will not move. If you are still feeling insecure, a little royal icing between the tiers will generally give extra peace of mind. Repeat the procedure for the next tier. Do remember to advise the caterers that the top tiers must be lifted upwards, and that they will not simply slide off.

Consider how you will disguise the edges of the tier boards – whether with piping, ribbon, a circlet of flowers, or think of bringing the covering icing down over it. No matter what you decide, it will be easier to achieve if you have planned for it in advance.

In America, these stacked cakes are usually made of sponge, so even four or five tiers is relatively light. However, if as is normal in Australia and England, you make it out of fruit cake, it will require strength to lift the finished cake. A smart decorator will do as much of the decorating as possible before the cakes are stacked, find a willing man to do the carrying, and check the cost of a hernia operation beforehand!

Fresh Flowers on Cakes

While the cake decorating purists may turn their noses up at this style of cake, it is a fact that many clients ask for fresh flowers, and so must be accommodated.

A row or two of ribbon with a shell piped border is the least risky trim for such cakes, as it will be little affected by the humidity produced by the moisture in the flowers, and would be difficult to accidentally damaged when arranging the flowers on the cake. However, it gives little opportunity for showing off your decorating abilities. I have found Chantilly Lace borders to be ideal, in that they are not as affected by humidity as normal lace pieces, and if accidentally touched, are far less likely to break. In most cases they make a perfect foil for fresh flowers.

In the past, decorators tended to leave the making of fresh flower sprays to appointed florists, not having the skills or confidence to attempt the job themselves

– often with disasterous results *(wet flowers eating the covering and melting away embroidery, or being far too big or tall etc)*. However, with the coming of edible discs, the scene has changed. If you can arrange icing flowers to your satisfaction, then you can also arrange fresh flowers - on discs.

For the cake pictured on page 71 I mixed a fair amount of Tylose powder with covering fondant, so that it would set quickly *(despite moisture from the flowers)*. The paste was then glued to the disc with Tylose glue. The Asparagus Fern and Fairy Statice have thin hard stems, so they were pushed straight into the fondant first. Because the roses had thick sappy stems, they were wired and taped, leaving two "prongs" to push into the fondant, and so stopped them from swivelling around. The orchid stems were not only sappy, but soft, so they also had to be wired and taped, although, as they were very

The bride's bouquet, the groom's boutonaire, and two gold rings form the decoration on this otherwise simple 11" round cake. The bouquet consists of champagne Roses and Agapanthus, tiny cream anonymous flowers, and very small forget-me-nots taped together to represent Gypsophila. Plenty of nice fine leaves, and cream ribbon loops, plus a few gold edged ribbons also went into the bouquet. It is held in place over the cake by a 6 inch length of 3/4 inch clear tubing pushed through to the board beneath, and packed with icing to the level of the cake. A wide cream ribbon edged with the gold trim ribbon used in the bouquet, and gold board edging form the finishing touches. This style of cake would be ideal to use with "Fresh Flowers".

light, a single stem of wire was sufficient. A few ribbons in a complimentary colour were added in the usual way. The sprays were made the night before the cake was required, but with careful preparation, could be made up to 48 hours in advance if necessary.

To keep the sprays looking really fresh, flowers must have had a chance to have a good drink first. Greenery should be soaked for several hours to thoroughly condition it, as well as clean off any dirt or insects. Once they have been made up, lay the individual arrangements on a flat surface such as a small plate or piece of cardboard, then place both in a plastic bag. Blow into the bag, filling it like a balloon, then tie it off securely. Surprisingly, flowers will last for days like this - they really like carbon dioxide. Place the flowers in the refrigerator, but avoid having it at the coldest setting, as some flowers will burn if subjected to really cold temperatures. If it can't be avoided, place a few sheets of newspaper on the shelf above them, as this stops the cold air sinking to the bottom of the fridge.

Many florists spray arrangements with preservative, and it really does help keep them looking fresh, but it also has a fairly strong odour, which could transfer to the cake icing, so I avoid it. Most commercially bought flowers have been sprayed with insecticide at some stage of their development, so try to keep them from direct contact with the cake as much as possible. Some clear plastic under the spray helps, or plenty of ribbon loops will also do the trick. My arrangments have a lot of fern at their base, which acts as a barrier, and as it came from my own garden, I know it to be spray free.

Eleven, eight and five inch tins were used for this fresh flower cake. The sprays which were arranged on edible discs contain Roses, Singapore orchids, Fairy Statice, Asparagus fern and ribbon loops. The rose pattern of the Chantilly Lace border was designed to match the roses in the sprays, and they were held in place with simple dot lace. I used eight pieces on the two bottom tiers, and only seven on the top tier, as eight would have made the pattern disproportionately small. The pillars were three inch, and the boards were flooded and finished with satin ribbon.

Quick & Easy Cakes

Sooner or later every cake decorator is asked for a cake in a hurry. With a few basic ground rules, some hints, and some lace and ribbon, you can turn the situation to your advantage. The old saying "less is more" is not only true, but quick and easy to achieve. Don't just throw things together, but work to a plan. By combining simple ideas with perfect workmanship, you can create a simply perfect cake!

Starting from the bottom up, the board should be as plain as possible (*I find flooding looks best*), but if time doesn't permit this, then choose the plainest paper possible for covering it. If the boards need an edging, keep it unobtrusive.

As there will be no fussy embroidery to hide mistakes, the cake covering must be well done. In order for your choice of ribbon and/or lace to sit nicely, the sides must be perpendicular, and not slope either in or out.

Try to select ribbons and laces that will compliment each other, and if it is a tiered cake, choose those that can be cut down in size if necessary.

Keep any pillars or stands as neat and simple as possible – try not to make a feature of them.

The flowers must be the best you can produce, whether they are in the form of a natural stem, or an arranged spray. If you choose a spray, try to stick to one type of flower, two at most.

Remember, in all facets of these cakes, the key word is simplicity.

Opposite   A narrow silver and white satin ribbon was used to edge the silver threaded lace that forms the side decoration for this elegant three tier hexagonal cake. The wired sprays consist of simple open roses, and bergundy coloured leaves (to match the bridesmaids gowns). Some deep pink ribbon loops add textural contrast, as well as transitional colour. The leaves were wired together in threes before being added to the sprays. The simplest of chrome stands was chosen to hold the cakes, which measured 10", 8" and 6".

Bible or Prayer Book

While there are a number of different techniques for making prayer books, I like to think mine is the easiest.

Start by cutting a piece of Polystyrene foam to the exact size you want the finished book. Roll out a piece of paste until it is large enough to form a cover for the piece of foam. *(I prefer to use some covering fondant such as Petinice or Regallce, and work in some tylose powder or Tylopur for this)*. Cut the rolled out paste to the correct width, and square off one end. Place the foam piece squarely on the trimmed end, then holding the paste in place carefully fold both over. Cut off the excess. Use your fingers to neaten all the edges, and then press a ruler *(or something with a straight edge)* down the left hand side to mark the spine.

Next you must either mark in the cross *(there are cutters available)*, or you can also wait until the cover is dry, and pipe or flood one. Or, you can cheat a little as I do, and buy a cheap jewellery pendant *(or earrings if it is a small bible)*, cut off the top loop with wire cutters, and press it into place on the cover. Once the cover has thoroughly dried, gently remove the foam piece, but replace it with something to act as a temporary support. Cut a small and equal amount off three sides of the foam *(one long side and the two short sides)*. Roll out a very thin strip of paste, and glue it to the three sides you have just trimmed, to represent the book pages. *(They should finish up just a little smaller than the cover)*. You can roll a smocking rolling pin along the edges if you have one, mark it with a knife, or simply leave it smooth. Whatever you choose, make sure that the icing doesn't creep over the edges, or it will be difficult to slip the "pages" back between the cover. Allow the edges to dry, then paint them with colour or gold as

you prefer. Once the paint is dry, slip the finished "pages" back between the covers with a little thin royal icing to hold it all together. If you plan a ribbon marker hanging from your book, glue it on to the pages before you put them into place.

As I said, a very simple method, with the use of the foam centrepiece keeping the finished book much lighter than a slab of icing would. Remember though, that in a competition the use of a jewellery cross would be classed as "an artificial or manufactured ornament" and as such could disqualify your cake. In this case, use the cross to press into the icing, remove it, and decorate the indentation it leaves later. Also, check to see that having a foam core will not disqualify your cake. If the answer is yes, then when making the pages, don't stick them to the foam. Allow them to dry in place around it, then when they are thoroughly dry, remove them from the foam, and glue them between the bible covers.

While this cake was designed for a small religious wedding, with the removal of the rings it would become suitable for an adult baptism or confirmation. Of course, without the bible and candle, the cake itself would be fitting for any number of special occasions. The same combination of Lisianthus, mock Agapanthus, and Heath were used on all three items. The flowers were arranged on a disc on the cake, and taped into a spray for the bible. The candle and flowers were both attached to a plaque made of covering fondant mixed with a small amount of Tylose powder, which meant the whole arrangement could be lifted off the stand for transportation. When attaching the lace to the cake, I placed it just above the line of the extension work, so that it would create an interesting scalloped edge. The large oval cake sits on a flooded board edged with satin ribbon. The bible measures 5" X 3-1/2" (13cms X 9cms), and the candle is 2" wide (5cms) and 8" tall (20cms). It is meant to be kept by the bride and groom, and re-lit on their wedding anniversary each year.

Vase or Urn

There will always be a place for an elegant vase or urn on wedding cakes. Unfortunately, there have been very few produced commercially, so here is an easy way to create your own.

You will need a bell mould for the bowl of the vase, plus something such as an egg-cup, with a base you can also use as a mould. Try to match both moulds if possible – a long narrow bell with a taller base, and a more squat base with a shorter bell. I got my original inspiration from the large sandstone garden urns on view at a nearby nursery, so gardening books and advertisements may help you with ideas.

Mould a bell and set it aside to dry. Mould a base piece, but make the bottom slightly concave. (As the paste dries it often swells a little, so if you take some out of the base, even if it does swell, it will still sit flat on the cake.) Leave the base to dry also. When both pieces can be freely handled, work up a small ball of paste to form the stem between the bell and the base. The easiest method is to simply place the ball of paste on the top of the base, and press the bell on to it. Remove the bell and leave the stem to dry before joining all three pieces together with melted moulding paste. Of course, if you are feeling creative then you can mould any shape you fancy for the stem. Should you decide on a fairly long stem, then it would be wise to build it round a core of spaghetti or even wire, as the finished vase will be quite heavy once it is filled with flowers. You can use your imagination to decorate the finished vase, with piping, lace pieces, edible glitter, or tiny moulded or cutter flowers – whatever takes your fancy.

Moulded Bells

The moulded bell used as the bowl of the vase pictured on the top of the American stacked cake is made with the same tecnique as for a hanging bell, regardless of size or shape.

First obtain a mould - mine are all off Christmas decorations, but you can usually find a selection of shapes and sizes at cake decorating outlets. As it is the inside of the bell that is used, any brands stamped on the plastic, or rough parts must be smoothed away. A sharp knife, followed by sandpaper is pretty effective. In order for the bell to balance upside down, I also cut away the hanging loop at the top. Wash and dry the bell thoroughly, then using a spare piece of paste, rub it all over the inside as hard as possible. Check the paste to see if it has been discoloured at all, and if not, your bell is ready for use. If the paste is discoloured, rub the inside as hard as possible with a soft cloth, then check again with the paste.

Cakes utilising two or more different shapes are always eye-catching, and this one is no different. I chose a large oval for the base, and a medium teardrop - which I cut down to make a little smaller – for the top. Although the board on the top tier appears to be only a little larger than the cake, it is much wider at the point where the flowers sit. As usual, the spray was formed on a disc, but without that little bit of extra width on the board, it would have been difficult to balance, and attach. As you can see, the spray consists of Roses (champagne and gerdo) Singapore Orchids, and mock Agapanthus and buds. To give the orchids a slight luminescent "glow", I brushed on the barest amount of Mother-of-Pearl Highlighter, before steaming them. The flowers were complimented by lots of leaves and ribbons, and the whole was taped with white to keep it looking light and dainty. The pillars measure 2-1/2", and I purposely used clear ones so that they wouldn't interfere with the line of the spray. The border was piped, then brush flooded using icing that had Mother-of-Pearl Highlighter mixed in, so that when dry, it would have a slight sheen to match the ribbon insertion. The addition of 2 rings on the top tier, and a boutonaire on the base cake, added the final touches. Just a tip - I stiffened the ribbon for the insertion with sugar solution, so that it would be easier to work with.

Moulded Bells
Continued

Coat the inside of the mould with a fine film of copha *(or solidified oil)*, followed by a generous dusting of cornflour. Take a good handful of paste, and work in some copha *(or solidified oil)*. You will find it far easier to make these bells if your paste is fairly soft, so use either very new paste which hasn't had time to firm up, or work a little moisture into older paste. Once it is thoroughly worked up, form it into a ball, cup it in one hand, and push the thumb of the other hand into the centre of it. With your thumb still in the middle, use your fingers to gently pull at the paste as you turn it round. Try and keep the outside as smooth as possible. When it is about half the size of your bell mould, dust the outside generously with cornflour, then drop it into the bell. Take a spare piece of paste, place it in the corner of a small freezer bag, or wrap a little plastic over it, and use this as a tool to rub the inside of the bell. Keep moving your wad of paste round and round, always forcing the bell paste towards the lip of the bell. Cut away the excess paste as it forms over the edge, and continue pressing and smoothing until you are satisfied that it is is thin enough. Check to see that the paste is not sticking to the bell, and cut off any that remains hanging over the lip. It really doesn't matter how thick the main body of the bell is, as long as the bottom edge is nice and fine, so run your plastic covered wad of paste round and round the edge until you have it as smooth and fine as possible.

If you have decided on a scalloped edge, then make yourself a cutter out of a wine bottle lid *(as I do)*, and press out the scallops. Use your wad of paste to smooth them off once they have been cut. Sieve some cornflour or icing sugar, and pack inside the bell with it, pressing it down firmly as you go. Level it off at the top, then lay a small board, or piece of heavy cardboard across it, and turn it over. Gently remove the outer mould, and check to see that the bell you have made is smooth and flawless. If it is flawed, replace the mould, empty out the packing, and press and work it until you feel you have rectified the problem. This way, your mould is ready for immediate re-use, and you don't have to wait two days for a bell to dry, only to find it is un-usable. *(Be warned however, if you use lumpy icing to pack your bell, you will end up with a dented one).*

When it is partly dry, use a pin or piece of wire to make a hanging hole at the top. If you are planning to decorate the bell with flowers, you can also make holes in the sides in which to insert the stems, which is neater than attaching them with dots of icing.

Wheelbarrow

W ith a little imagination, an icing wheelbarrow can be every bit as useful to a cake decorator, as a real one is to a gardener. By varying the colour and its contents, it can be made to suit all sorts of celebration cakes. Apart from the obvious things, such as filling it with flowers for a feminine cake, or vegetables for man, there is no end to the things it can contain. Do you know a choc-o-holic who could resist a barrow full of chocolate peanuts, or a child who wouldn't love one full of tiny sweets (*especially if their name was spelt out in the same lollies*)? A Christmas cake sporting a barrow loaded with presents, or holly and pine cones, looks quite festive, and one brimming with small eggs, and surrounded by chickens or rabbits fills the bill for Easter. The possibilities are endless, it is just a matter of letting your imagination loose.

Bright Ideas

For Australian Cake Decorating

A wheelbarrow, overflowing with tiny pine cones and holly leaves, conveys the Christmas spirit on this medium oval cake. The barrow was made white, then painted with a brown alcohol mix for a rustic look. The greeting was brush flooded. Red and green holly embroidery, plus double dropped decorate the sides, and a bright red ribbon finished the flooded board.

Wheelbarrow
Continued

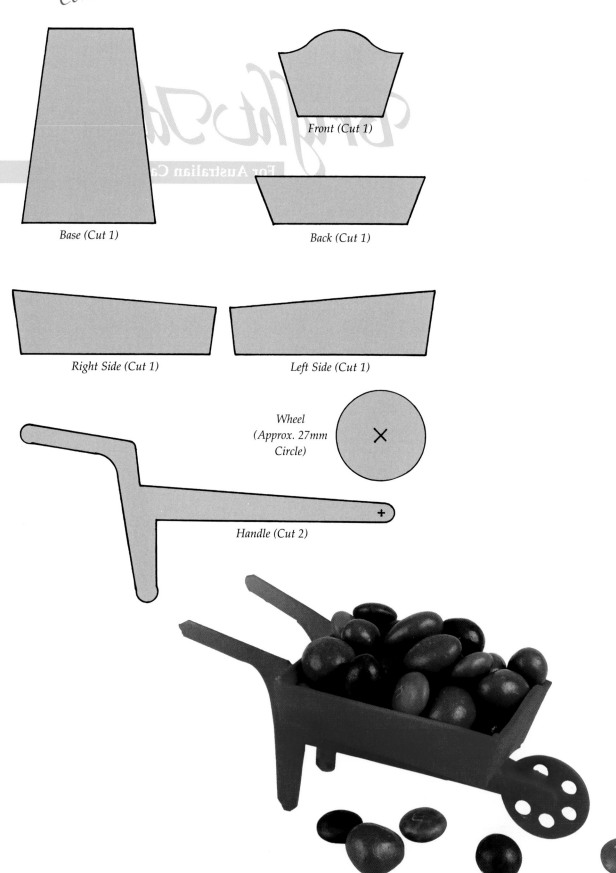

Base (Cut 1)

Front (Cut 1)

Back (Cut 1)

Right Side (Cut 1)

Left Side (Cut 1)

Wheel
(Approx. 27mm
Circle)

Handle (Cut 2)

Wheelbarrow
Continued

Rather than use moulding paste, I prefer to mix a small amount of Tylose powder with my normal covering fondant. It is more economical, sets very hard, and is easy to work with.

The pattern pieces will fit best if your paste is rolled fairly thin, but if you have made your pieces thicker or thinner, then it is fairly easy to rub the pieces along some fine sandpaper *(glasspaper)* till they do fit. You may also wish to reduce or enlarge the pattern using a photocopier, but remember that in order to make the pieces fit, they will have to be thicker or thinner *(as the case may be)*.

For a more feminine cake, use a tiny heart or blossom cutter to cut pieces out of the sides of the wheelbarrow.

I have taken to cutting out two sets of pieces at a time, which means you won't be caught out if you happen to break a piece, and you can make a barrow up in a hurry if need be.

To make strong joins when assembling the barrow, it is best to use melted moulding paste. To make easy work of it, place a small piece of paste, along with a drop or two of water, into the corner of a plastic bag, and tie it off. Melt the paste either in the microwave oven, or by sitting the bag in hot water for a minute or two. Once melted, work the corner of the bag between your fingers until you feel that the water and paste are mixed, then cut off just the corner of the bag, and you can then pipe along all the join lines. A damp brush will keep the joins looking neat and smooth.

Rather than use coloured icing, I make my barrow in white, and paint on any colour later, using a mix of food colouring and alcohol. As well as leaving you free to make last minute colour changes, it can also produce a more rustic look.

Cut out all the pieces as accurately as possible, and set aside to thoroughly dry. See the instructions for the Flower Barrow on page 87 for making fancy wheels.

If you don't mind a little extra work, use a piping tube to cut a small hole in the centre of the wheel, as well as corresponding holes in the shafts. Cut a short length of wire or satay stick to act as an axle when assembling the pieces.

Directions for Assembling the Wheelbarrow

Start by placing the base piece on a non stick surface *(freezer wrap or greaseproof paper)*.

The side pieces attach to the SIDE EDGES of the base, with the wide ends towards the front of the barrow. The sides should be level with the base at the back, and protrude past the base at the front.

The front piece also attaches to the SIDE EDGE of the base, and also to the INSIDE of the sides. Note that they are meant to be angled, not vertical.

The back is attached to the TOP of the base, and also the INSIDE edges of the sides *(in other words it fits inside the framework created by the other pieces)*.

As you will probably be filling the barrow, it is not necessary for the inside joins to be too neat. In fact, any extra paste over them can only help to make them stronger. Make sure though, that outside joins that will show, are wiped over with a damp brush, to remove any excess paste. Leave to dry.

When it can be safely handled, rest the upturned tray of the barrow on something, so that you can glue on the handles and wheel. Again, on the two insides of the handles that go under the barrow, you can use extra joining paste, as it will not show once the barrow is upright, but make sure that the joins that will show are neatly finished. Join the wheel in place at the same time. If you are planning anything heavy in the barrow, make sure that the wheel is thoroughly glued into place, as all the weight will be on this one point. Give it plenty of time to dry, and support it while you are arranging anything in it, or the wheel may give way.

To secure the barrow to your cake, make two small shallow slits in the icing, fill them with a little royal icing, and rest the legs in them. Use a damp brush to smooth away any icing that bulges up, and your barrow will be invisibly glued to the cake top.

Christmas Owls

For a quick, easy and effective Christmas decoration you can't beat these cute little marzipan owls. They can be used on cakes, or set on plaques for gifts or as table decorations.

Knead a ping-pong ball sized piece of marzipan (*approximately 40gm*) until it is quite soft, then form a ball and roll the paste between the palms of both hands until it is very shiny. At this stage it is ready to be transformed into an owl.

Still using the palms of your hands, form the ball into a slight pear shape - minus the waist. Use your fingers to pull two "ears" (*in reality they are only longer feathers*) from the top of the pear shape. Press both thumbs in the area below the ears to form eye spaces. With a sharp knife create the wings by making a fairly deep curved cut on each side, and flare it out at the base.

Turn the owl upside down, and working from the front to the back, slice about 3/4 of the way through the base, then fold this flap backwards to form a tail. Sit the owl on a board and use your knife to mark feathers on the tail piece.

Cut two small circles of paper, and stick them over the eye spaces with a touch of water. Next airbrush the owl with brown food colouring, avoiding the front breast area, which should stay uncoloured. If you prefer to use chalks, then you will need to leave the owl to dry and become firm, before adding his colouring.

Once you are satisfied that the colouring is right, remove the paper eye patches, and the owl is ready for the finishing touches.

Roll two tiny balls of yellow icing for eyes, moisten one side and press them into place in the eye spaces. With a fine brush and black food colouring, paint an iris on each.

Colour a small piece of paste red, form a Father Christmas style hat, and attach in place on the owl with a little moisture. Use a small "O" size tube or paper bag to pipe white royal icing "fur" round the rim, plus a fluffy ball on the tip.

Tint a small amount of royal icing orange or yellow, and pipe the beak directly on the owl by first piping a dot, then forming a larger one above it, and pulling it out and over the first one. Finish with a point.

Mark where the owl is to sit, pipe two sets of 3 toes, then sit the owl over them, so that they peek out from beneath his chest.

Top *Christmas Owls are the perfect subjects for mini cakes – in this case a five inch round. Some holly, and a jaunty tartan ribbon and bow adds just the right festive touch.*

Bottom *The message "Guess hooo's 50" on this medium oval birthday cake could be changed to suit any number of special occasions. While this owl is bare-headed, any appropriate hat would personalise the cake. Imagine for instance a tam-o-shanter for a Scot, or a helmet for a policeman, soldier, or construction worker, or even a beanie and scarf in favourite sports team colours – there is always some sort of adornment that is topical and suitable. I chose a stem of gum leaves and nuts to sit the marzipan owl on, but a branch with any combination of leaves, berries, nuts or fruits would look just as good. As you can see, I have adapted my Universal Border to suit, and edged it with brown ribbon, which has been repeated around the board edge.*

Christmas Owls
Continued

Remember, you can add character to your owl by controlling the initial shape. ie: short and fat, or long and thin. The wings can be left almost straight, or the tips flipped outward for a jaunty look. The ears can stick out on a slightly upward angle, be straight, or curved, or droop downward. When cutting the paper eye patches, they can be circular or oval, and also be angled either both leaning to one side, or tilting in at the top or bottom. Even the hat can add character - try making it too small, extra long so it drags on the ground, or so big it slips over one eye. When you add the eye yellows and paint the irises, imagine a point at which the owl is looking, and make and paint them accordingly, so the owl will actually be saying something.

With these tips, and a little forethought, your Christmas Owl will be a real hoot!

Elegance is the keyword for this 3 tiered wedding cake. The bride's gown featured silk roses, so the theme was carried through not only the sprays on the cake, but also included on the Chantilly Lace border. The tulle bells which crown the cake were ringed with a circle of basic blossom cut-outs, piped with cornelli, then sprayed with Design Master Glitter Silver to give a romantic look. The tiny orchids and small mauve blossoms that nestled among the Rose sprays were repeated in the arrangement above the bells, with long trailing ribbons for a softening effect. The cakes were 11 inch, 8 inch, and 5 inch, with 3-1/2inch pillars and flooded boards. There are eight lace pieces on the two bottom cakes, but only seven on the top tier, as eight would have meant making the pattern disproportionately small.

* DESIGN MASTER Glitter Silver (or Glitter Gold or Pearl) is a professional florists' spray. Obviously it can't be eaten, and as a consequence, should only ever be used on articles which are OBVIOUSLY inedible, such as tulle ornaments. Articles should be sprayed well away from cakes, and once dry, use a fine soft brush to remove any loose flecks that otherwise might fall on to the cake. If you are uncomfortable with using the spray, there are excellent edible glitter products available. To use them on tulle ornaments, I brush the ornament with clear alcohol solution then quickly sprinkle on the glitter before it can dry. Larger ornaments need to be done in stages.

Tulle Ornaments

The response to the tulle ornaments featured in my previous book has been so positive, that I have decided to include one or two new ideas for you to try. As I wrote before, it is not really tulle that is used, but COTTON MOSQUITO NET. The same basic rules apply also. When greasing moulds always use white shortening, such as copha or lard - never butter, which will ultimately stain. Only a light coat is required, and place the prepared mould in the refrigerator till ready for use.

When stiffening tulle, always use hot solution - reheat any mixture that has gone cold.

Always blot off any excess mixture with a towel, kitchen paper, or a barely damp sponge, to avoid sugary build-up on the dried ornament. If you do find your dried tulle has clogged with sugar, simply use a pin to break the pieces out. Boring work, but better than wasting an ornament.

A damp sponge is best for patting the tulle into place on a mould.

Once dry, the warmth of your hand is normally enough to release an ornament from its' mould, but should this fail, a pin slipped under the tulle here and there will usually shift a stubborn one.

Ornaments which are cut out of flat tulle are easier to manage if you tie pieces together at the corners. It is a simple matter to thread a length of white cotton through matching holes on either piece, tie with a double knot, then cut off the loose ends as short as possible. This way, joins, once cornellied will be invisible, and your ornaments will not only be stronger, but will appear to have been made in one piece. Take care not to pull the knots so tight that the pieces overlap, they should always just meet.

Stiffening tulle is an incredibly sticky business, so I usually gather up all my moulds and make as many shapes as possible at the one time. The tulle shapes will last indefinitely if stored in a dry place, and you will find them very useful for rush jobs. Likewise, it is handy to stiffen as large a piece as possible when preparing for an ornament that is made from a flat piece of tulle. I store these spare pieces between the pages of a book.

There are different grades of tulle available, based on the number of holes to the square inch. The problem arises as to which to use for what. As a general guide, I use the finer tulle (the most holes) for flat pieces, or over moulds that are not too intricate. For bells, slippers, swans and the like, you will find success easier if you use a coarser tulle (fewer, bigger holes). The bigger the holes, the more "give" and stretch you can rely on.

Cream tulle is available, but if you are caught out, a dash of tea or coffee in the stiffening solution will do the trick.

Finally, when doing the piped cornelli work, try to work against a dark background with a good light, or you will find yourself literally going cross-eyed.

Opposite A tulle flower cart, filled with small blooms in various shades of violet, is the focal point on this medium long – octagonal cake. With such a simple top, there was room for a more intricate, or heavy border. To achieve the look I wanted, I used two rows of flooded lace between two rows of ribbon. A small mauve blossom at the base of each piece of lace added extra colour and dimension. To make the lace go round the corners I piped a dot of royal icing on each point, and just pressed it onto the cake. Although it snapped in parts, it stayed in place, and the breaks were not noticeable. While not really visible in the photo, the cart had a slight dusting of edible glitter sprinkled over it, as a touch of glamour.

Flower Barrow

What could be sweeter on a birthday cake than a tulle flower barrow? Inspiration for this decoration came from a commercially available plastic barrow, and you will find it useful to have one on hand when making the tulle version. The brolly can be used as a mould, and your flowers can be arranged in the barrow itself, and then transferred to the tulle ornament when set, which will reduce the chances of breakage.

Cut out all the pattern pieces roughly, and use them to establish how much tulle you will need to stiffen *(see page 90)*. Remember to allow for shrinkage. While the tulle is soaking in the stiffening solution, grease a flat surface on which to dry it. *(I use a piece of acrylic board, but you could just as easily use your kitchen bench top. By doing it last thing at night, it will be dry by morning, and can be lifted before causing anyone any inconvenience).* Remove the tulle with

tweezers once it is thoroughly saturated, and blot off any excess with a towel or damp sponge. Lay the tulle out flat, pulling evenly at the edges till you see that all the little holes are the same shape - you don't want some pieces to have oval holes while other parts have round ones. Once it looks fairly even, take a piece of freezer paper or waxed lunchwrap, lay it on top of the tulle, and proceed to flatten it all nicely. Check again to see that it is all even, with the edges as smooth as possible, *(some bunching and puckering is inevitable)*, then carefully remove the top paper and allow the tulle to dry thoroughly.

While the tulle is drying, prepare the wheels by cutting out two, one inch circles of moulding paste. They can be left plain, or made more decorative by cutting pieces out of them, or gluing cut-out shapes on to them, the choice is yours. For the ones pictured I first cut a daisy shape out of the centre of the

Flower Barrow
Continued

wheels, then glued a small circle of paste into the middle of the daisy shape *(to represent the axle)*. I always cut out an extra wheel in case of accidents. Leave them on a flat surface to dry.

Once the tulle is dry, carefully pin the main pattern piece firmly underneath the tulle, with the pattern markings visible. Cut out as accurately as possible, then remove all but one pin from the centre of the barrow base. Lay a ruler along the front fold line, and bend the tulle upwards, exactly on the line, making as sharp a fold as possible. Repeat on the side and back fold lines. Un-pin the pattern, and using white cotton thread, and double knots, tie all four corners together. It is easiest to use a needle, and don't pull the knots too tight, the edges should just meet. Also, watch that you push the thread through a complete hole, not one that has been partially cut. Cut off any loose ends. I have also tried glueing the edges of models together with craft glue, but have the found the most successful method is to first tie knots, then add a tiny dab of glue over them for security. Next, fold a small piece of the stiffened tulle in half, place the narrow end of the leg pattern against the fold, and cut out *(2 pieces joined at the base)*. Place the ruler along the fold line, and bend back one piece of tulle. Turn the leg over, and with the ruler, bend back the other side of the leg piece. These two folded "wings" should be attached to the underside of the barrow *(where the cross is marked on the pattern)*. You can sew the leg in place, or take the easy way out and use craft glue. If you are planning to put large numbers of flowers in the barrow, it may be wise to run a fine white covered wire between the two pieces of tulle. Make it double, and folded over either side the same as the leg itself. Once cornellied, the wire becomes almost invisible.

For the Brolly

If you have the plastic barrow, then you can use the brolly as a mould. If not, cut out a piece of flat stiffened tulle using the pattern supplied. Join the two straight edges together with double knots. To use the plastic brolly mould, first grease it, then put in the refrigerator while you soak the tulle in stiffening solution. Once it has absorbed enough of the mix, remove it with tweezers and blot off any excess moisture. Retrieve the mould from the fridge, and drape the damp tulle over it. Pull it fairly tightly, and fold it over the edges and into the centre of the brolly. You can fill it with coins or similar to hold the edges down and keep the tulle tight over the shape. When dry, cut along the edges, and remove the stiffened brolly.

Fit a piping bag with a 00 tube, fill with Royal Icing, and cornelli all over the outside of the barrow. When you come to corners make a point of going back and

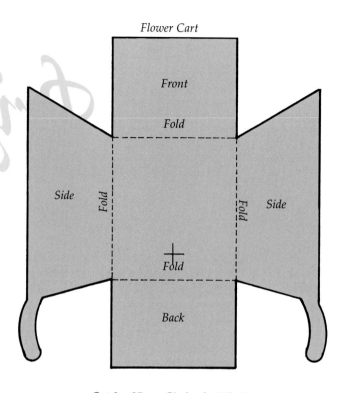

Flower Cart

Cut 2 x 27mm Circles for Wheels

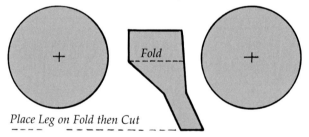

Place Leg on Fold then Cut

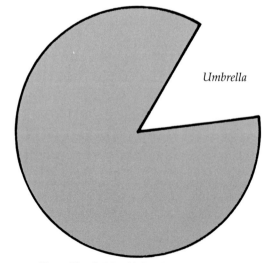

Umbrella

Use a Plastic Mould for the Umbrella or cut 66 mm Circle as shown

forth from one side to the other to keep them neat and add strength. Cornelli the brolly.

When all the components are dry, you can begin assembly. Glue the wheels in place using melted moulding paste for preference. The best way to do this is to place the wheel face down on your board, put your choice of glue on the wheel, and lay the side of the barrow on it. Use a matchbox or something similar to butt up to the wheel base, ensuring that it is aligned so that the barrow leg is just a fraction longer. When this wheel has dried in place, turn over, and repeat for the other wheel, again using a box to check that the wheels will be level. This way both wheels will be straight, and not at an angle, which will give your barrow a rickety look. By leaving the leg just a bit longer, when it comes to attaching to the cake, you can make a small slit in the covering fondant, fill it with a touch of melted moulding paste, and sit the leg into it. Push it down until the cart itself is perfectly level. Use a slightly damp brush to smooth over any icing that may bulge upwards, and once dry, the cart will be held firmly, and invisibly, in place.

If you have the plastic barrow, then place a small amount of paste in the centre of it. Tape or ribbon a piece of thick wire, or a satay stick, and insert this in the centre to form the stem of the brolly. Check from different angles to see that it is perpendicular, then fill the barrow with your choice of ribbons and flowers. Check that the stem is straight one last time, then glue the brolly on top. Wait until all is firmly set, then transfer the entire arrangement into the tulle barrow. Use a touch of "glue" to make sure that it can't move later. If you don't have the plastic cart, then support the tulle cart on something that will keep the wheels off the ground while you add the flowers and brolly.

Stiffening Recipe

The recipe for stiffening "tulle" is simple, provided you remember that it is not nylon tulle that you work with but COTTON NET.

Mix three parts of ordinary white sugar (the kind you stir into your tea), with one part of water. Heat the mix – either in a microwave or on the stove – until it comes to the boil. Remove from the heat and stir until the liquid becomes perfectly clear. Use while still very hot, and reheat if it cools.

OR

1 teaspoon of starch granules

50 mls boiling water

Put the starch into a small container such as a Vegemite jar. Add just enough cold water to mix it to a paste, then add the boiling water and stir until the mix turns semi clear. Use while still hot. You may have to adjust this recipe a little depending on the type of starch you use.

The medium diamond cake was designed to form the centrepiece for a Christmas table. Small white blossoms, holly leaves and berries, white and silver ribbons, and three taper candles make up the centre spray. The arrangement was formed separately on a small plague, and put in place after the extension work was finished and dry. Because of the extra weight of the candles it was necessary to incorporate a small support in the centre of the extension work. The straight line for the side extension was achieved by attaching pieces of pre-cut and dried paste to the sides of the cake. I also graduated the lace, so that it matched the tapered extension. Small holly embroidery, and ribbon that finished in a bow amid a spray of holly at each end of the cake, were the finishing touches.

Tulle Hat

A pretty ornament for a birthday cake, or wedding top, tulle hats are easy to make. You will need a shape to form the crown of the hat over, and what you use will determine the ultimate size of the hat. My favourite mould is half of a christmas ornament, but you can use a ping-pong or golf ball, or if you are absolutely desperate, the roundest end of an egg. Whatever your mould, rub it generously with copha or solidified oil, and put it in the fridge while you soak the tulle. When the tulle has fully absorbed the stiffening solution, take it out, and blot off any excess moisture. Stretch the tulle over the mould. If it is a half shape, then tuck the excess net into the centre of the mould and hold it down with a few coins until it dries. If you are using a complete ball shape, then pull the paste over the ball, and hold it in place underneath by twisting a rubber band around it. If your net won't stretch that far, then a rubber band at the widest point will do, or sit the ball in a "V" shaped medicine glass to keep the tulle tight until it dries. If you have resorted to using an egg, then use an egg cup.

Stiffen a flat piece of tulle for the brim, and set it aside to dry. Next cut a paper pattern for the brim. It should be big enough to suit the crown you have made. Cut a smaller circle out of it to accommodate the crown. Make it slightly off centre, as the front of the brim should be wider than the back. When cutting the hole, remember that the crown is not too high, in fact it should only be about one third to one quarter the height of the ball, not half. When the flat tulle is dry, cut out the brim from your pattern and fit it over the crown *(still on its mould)*. Pull the brim down at the front, so that viewed from the side it has a slightly downward curve at the front, and is not completely flat. Pin it gently, front and back, on to the lower half of the crown, and with needle and cotton, overstitch the two pieces together. Start at the point where you plan your decorations, so any knots or finishing touches of glue will be easy to hide. Remove the pins, and ease the crown from the mould. Cut away the excess tulle from under the brim. Finish with piped cornelli work, making sure you go back and forth over the join to hide it. If you plan to have a ribbon around the crown, put it in place before you cornelli, or it will not sit flat. Decorate around the crown with flowers and bows. For a brides hat, you may like to try a ruffle and tails of soft transparent organza ribbon.

Troubleshooting

Anyone who has made more than one decorated cake has made some mistakes, and as I have made my fair share of both, here are a few of the solutions I have used.

CHALK ON A CAKE SURFACE: I accidentally spilt a container of green chalk over the top of a finished cake. Fortunately, the spray was on an edible disc, so I was able to remove it and give myself "room to move". The solution was to blow off as much of the chalk as possible, then I used cotton wool balls soaked in clear alcohol to wipe off what was left – starting at the outside of the stain of course, and changing the cotton ball after only one wipe. When the colour was removed, I then wiped over the whole top of the cake, dusted on some sifted icing sugar, and rubbed it all over the cake surface, so that if the texture was in any way changed, it would not show up as a patch. The cake is featured in this book, and I defy you to find which one!

For a small stain, *(of any sort)*, after cleaning with the alcohol try rubbing just the damp area with sifted icing sugar, rather than the entire cake top.

POLLEN ON DARK STAMENS: The problem was that I wanted small dark flowers *(achieved by dipping)*, but fancied yellow tips on the stamens. The solution was to use blank stamens, then once the dipped flowers had dried, I gently tipped each one with some very thick *(almost jelly-like)* Tylose glue, then dipped the stamen tips into yellow chalk. The result was so natural that I am using the idea on more that just dark flowers now. Occasionally, a little of the chalk will fall back onto the flower, just as pollen sometimes drops onto flower petals, and if it does, I leave it there, rather than brush it away.

A DIFFERENT SIZE TIN: The problem was that I fancied a cake in a slightly different sized tin than was available. Rather than cook a bigger cake and cut it down, I decided to alter the tin. It was easy to make a piece of thick cardboard the right size to shorten the tin. I covered it with foil, and also made two smaller pieces *(also foil covered)* to wedge it into place. The cake cooked perfectly, and the cardboard underneath the foil was unaffected.

TEARDROP TINS: Just a word to the wise if you are about to purchase teardrop tins. Look for those that consist of the sides only, and have to be used on a tray or in a larger tin. These are best because you can turn them over and reverse the shape if you fancy. Don't forget when cooking in them that they should be the reverse of the way you want the finished cakes to be. If you feel confident enough, you can make a teardrop shape by cutting a piece out of the front of an oval cake.

RIBBON ON BOARD EDGES: Narrow double-sided tape seems to give the best finish when trimming the edge of a board with ribbon, but if it is unavailable, the next best solution is to use stick glue. Just rub the stick on to the edge of the board, then press the ribbon on. If you have to handle the board immediately, just watch that you don't push the ribbon out of place, as it takes a while to dry.

KEEPING CANDLES STRAIGHT: The tall taper candles that I have used on a number of the cakes pictured in this book invariably start to twist once they are made to stand upright for more than a day or two. To keep them from doing so, use lengths of covered wire to hold them straight. Make a circle of wire, drop it down over one candle, then give the wire a twist or two before circling it around the second one. It will take at least two, sometimes three of these to impose your will on them. Don't forget to remove the wires before the cake goes on show!

CURLED EDGES: During workshops and classes, so many people have indicated their disappointment that their flowers never look quite the same as mine. In most cases it is because I flute on my fingers, as opposed to doing it on a board *(except for very big flowers)*. If you try fluting some paste while resting it on your fingers, you will see that it makes just the very edge of the paste curl up a little. When the petals are turned over, that slight curl gives them a softer more natural look. I also feel that you have more control over the pressure you apply to the fluting if it is done on your fingers. If you are not used to it, then it will take practice and patience, but the results will justify your efforts.

PUTTING A GLISTEN ON FLOWERS: Many flowers when viewed in a good light seem to glisten – just little specks here and there that give it a special glow. I have found that the best way to achieve that same look is to mix a small amount of ivory or mother of pearl HI-LITER into a container of potato flour. This mix can be brushed on to a flower before steaming, and the result is excellent. Much of the HI-LITER disappears with the steaming, leaving just enough to look natural. For really dark colours it is best to use the deeper coloured HI-LITERS.

CUTTING OUT PETALS: When you roll out moulding paste, especially if it is a fairly large piece, then the edges will always be thinnest. I take advantage of this, by angling my cutters so that the outside edges of the petals are cut from the outside edge of the paste, leaving the thickest part in the middle where it is not so obvious, and is actually useful. After cutting a circle of petals out, I then re-roll the bit that is left in the middle again, and cut out another row. It is an easy habit to get into, and one that will pay dividends.

CRUSTY BITS ON PASTE: After making a new batch of paste, and setting it aside in a plastic bag, I often found that if I didn't use it fairly soon, when I unwrapped it, there would be some crustiness on the outside. Now, as soon as my paste has cooled and set, I remove it from the bag, rub copha or solidified oil all over it, and put it in a new bag to keep. This is also useful if you know you won't be using the paste for a while, as the copha seems to set up an airtight barrier, and it keeps better.

WRITING ON CAKES: I have never had a problem with writing in icing on cakes *(just draw a line with white chalk, squeeze the piping bag with the left hand, and hold the tube and write with it as you would a pen. Brush the chalk line off with a stiff brush later).* However, sometimes, one just feels like a change. A friend advised buying a lettering book, and tracing then transferring the words I wanted on to the cakes. It works a treat, as you can see by some of the cakes in this book. Some I brush flooded, and for some I filled a piping bag with thin royal icing and pressure piped the words. With this method the writing can be placed exactly where you want it, and nothing is left to chance.

Recipes

Moulding Paste

250g icing sugar (8 Ozs)
30ml water (1 oz)
2 scant teaspoons gelatine
1 rounded teaspoon liquid glucose

Sift icing sugar into a bowl. Measure water into a small bowl or cup and sprinkle with the gelatine. When it has been absorbed stand in a saucepan of hot water and dissolve gently. Once it has completely dissolved add the glucose. When the liquid is clear and free of any lumps add it to the icing sugar, stirring with a knife. Store the mixture in a plastic bag and seal in an airtight container. The mix needs to stand for at least eight hours before use. Remove it from the bag, and rub Copha or solidified oil all over the outside of the paste before replacing it in a clean new bag. This not only helps keep air from the paste, but if left in the original bag for too long, when you remove it there can sometimes be a slight crustiness on the outside

In very hot weather I add just a little more gelatine, and an extra ounce of icing sugar, which makes a much firmer paste. If you have naturally hot hands, you might also find it a help.

Stiffening

RECIPE 1

3 parts sugar
1 part water

Stir over heat until mix comes to the boil. Remove from heat immediately and continue stirring till all sugar grains have dissolved. Use while hot. Store in sealed container in refrigerator. Reheat before next use.

If you a have a microwave, then you can make very small amounts and use it fresh each time *(1 tsp of water to 3 tsp of sugar)*.

RECIPE 2

1 teaspoon of starch granules
50 mls boiling water

Put the starch into a small container such as a Vegemite jar. Add just enough cold water to mix it to a paste, then add the boiling water and stir until the mix turns semi clear. Use while still hot.

This recipe works beautifully on the brand of starch I use, but if you find that it is not quite right for you, then simply follow the instructions for stiff hot water starching on the packet you have.

In an emergency, both of the above recipes will dry perfectly under a hair dryer, provided the mould you are using will stand the heat.

Edible shine for leaves

RECIPE 1

1 part Gum Arabic (Acacia Gum)
3 parts water

Put water in a small bowl or cup and sprinkle with the Gum Arabic. Stand in a pot of water and boil until the gum has dissolved. To use, keep on a gentle boil, and take the leaves to the stove. The mix dries very quickly, so you must work deftly and fairly fast. Use a brush wide enough to cover the leaves so they are done in one stroke. If you want to chalk leaves first, it must be done when the modelling paste is soft, and rubbed well in, otherwise when you paint on the gum you will wipe off the chalk at the same time. Store in an airtight container in the refrigerator and re-boil it when next required. It is advisable to make only a small amount at a time

RECIPE 2

1 tsp gelatine
1 tsp liquid glucose
2 desertspoons water

Put the water in a cup or small container and sprinkle over the gelatine. When absorbed, stand in a pot of water and heat until dissolved. Add the liquid glucose, and stir well. Keep the mix warm while painting leaves. Store in sealed container in the refrigerator and re-heat to use. Holly berries can also be dipped in shine for an extra glossy look, as can blueberries, blackberries etc.

Quick alternative

Alternately, paint on egg white. Use two coats, allowing the first to dry before applying the second. This method is not as long lasting as the gum arabic or gelatine, and produces more a waxy look, rather than shine.

Tylose glue

1/4 teaspoon Tylose powder (Tylopure)
50 mls water

Sprinkle the powder over the water and allow to soak – if you are in a hurry, then stirring will speed up the process. If you can measure out half of a 1/4 teaspoon, then make half the amount, as 50 mls will be more than the average decorator requires. Add extra water if too thick, or a pinch extra powder if you wish to thicken the glue.

Embroidery & Lace

Small Heart Top Embroidery

Large Heart Top Embroidery

Reverse patterns for opposite sides of heart, and add more space between sprays

Embroidery & Lace
Continued

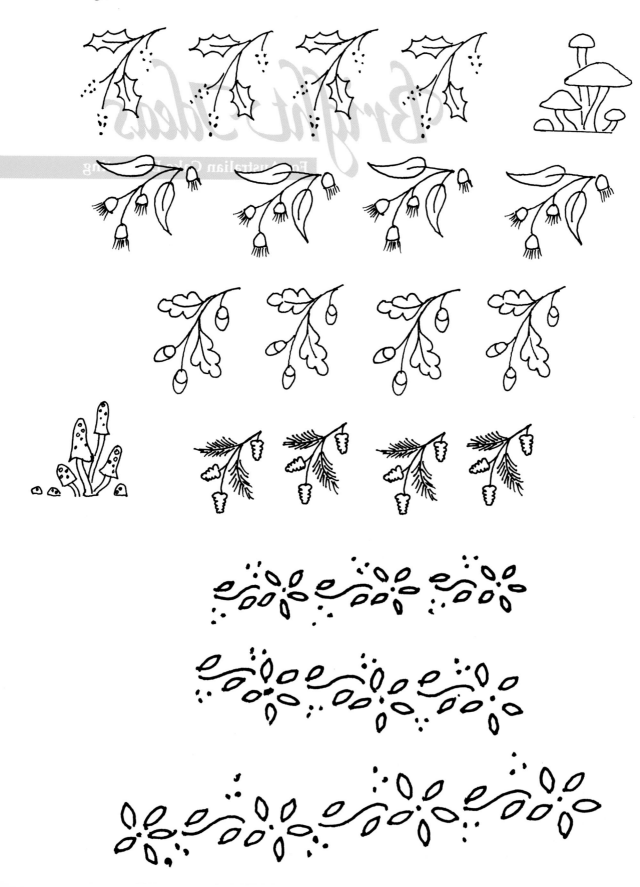

Embroidery & Lace
Continued

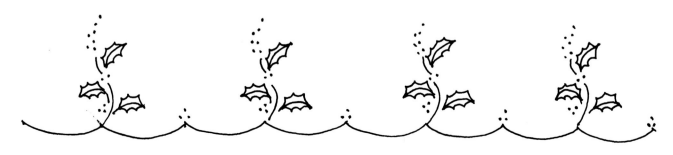

Embroidery & Lace
Continued